Alvin Gibbs has been a performing and recording musician since the punk explosion of the late seventies, working with a number of bands, most notably the UK Subs. Since touring with Iggy Pop in the eighties, he has worked all over the world, rejoining the UK Subs in the late nineties. Gibbs is the author of *Destroy: The Definitive History of Punk Rock*. He is currently working on a film script and a novel.

For Trine
with all my love

Neighbourhood threat
on tour with iggy pop

ALVIN GIBBS

Neighbourhood Threat
On Tour With Iggy Pop

by Alvin Gibbs

Revised edition published in 2001 by
Codex Books, PO Box 148, Hove, BN3 3DQ, UK
www.codexbooks.co.uk

ISBN 1 899598 17 0

First published by Britannia Press Publishing, 1995

Codex Books would like to express its sincere gratitude to the contributing
photographers. Every effort has been made to contact the contributors to
obtain permission to use their work in this new edition, though not always
with success. If your photographs appear in this edition and we have been
unable to contact you, please get in touch.

Graphic design by Surface Impression Ltd
Printed in Canada by Westcan Printing Group

INTRO

Picture this. A yellow cab speeds away from Kennedy Airport, NYC in the year of our Lord 1981. I'm in the back seat in a state approaching ecstasy watching every aspect from my window as America becomes a reality.

It was my first time in America, my first time in the Holy Land of rock 'n' roll. What's more I'd made it there as a touring musician in British punk rock band the UK Subs. Together, in a fleet of taxis, we were accelerating to the most exciting place on Earth; the island of Manhattan. As we crossed the Brooklyn Bridge we saw her laid out before us. What grandeur and grace. Though I had seen the great capitals of Europe, I'd never seen anything like this. The magnificence of Manhattan took my breath away.

We drove through the canyons of the city to the Hotel Iroquois, a West 44th St hostelry with a rock 'n' roll pedigree. In the hotel bar later that evening I was drinking bourbon with the drummer when a man entered the room and got himself a beer. I was too deep in conversation, too high on the realisation of where I was, to really notice him. The bar was dimly lit. As he made his way to the exit he tripped over my protruding legs and stumbled to the floor, his beer crashing onto our table demolishing the drinks. I helped him to his feet and apologised. He gave us a half smile, looked at the shattered glass and spilt liquor and muttered, "Shit happens."

After ordering another beer, he kind of tip-toed out of the door and disappeared into the hotel lobby. Sitting at an adjacent table, a Subs' roadie with sharper eyes and a better memory for faces than I, came over and asked, "Do you know who you just sent to his knees with those lethal Chelsea boots of yours?"

"Ain't got a clue," I answered.

He took a long draw on his cigarette to heighten the suspense. "That, my boy, was Iggy Pop."

That was my first, inauspicious meeting with the man Iggy. It would be some years before we would meet again.

In many ways, Iggy Pop was the reason I was in a band sitting in that bar in New York City in the first place. Along with the New York Dolls, Iggy Pop and the Stooges had been deeply influential to me. In the early 70s, when the pompous dirges of so-called 'Progressive Rock' groups were all the rage, the Dolls and the Stooges were a revelation. This was no quaalude music. This was music with attitude. Amphetamines were the drug of choice when listening to those gunslingers.

As the decade moved on, they in turn spawned a new generation. The Punk Rock explosion. The raw guitars, swagger and savvy of The Clash and Sex Pistols owed much to Iggy. It was at this time I picked up the bass guitar. I liked the subversive nature of the instrument and taught myself to play by listening and learning the basslines from a bunch of favourite records that included the Stooges' *Funhouse* and *Raw Power* albums. Hooking up with The Users, The Physicals and ex-Damned guitarist Brian James for gigging experience, I went on to join the UK Subs during the dying embers of 1979.

Those were the halcyon days. Four years of world touring. Hundreds of nights of adrenaline-fuelled, fast, loud music and a reckless, outlaw lifestyle.

We sold records in decent numbers, even getting to appear on that British TV institution, *Top of the Pops,* on several occasions. In turn, we were to influence future bands like Guns N' Roses who listened to the Subs' music at their onset and would later go on to record a version of one of our songs, 'Down On The Farm', for their own *Spaghetti Incident?* album.

We were the first punk band ever to get to play behind the Iron Curtain in Poland after the then-dictator General Jaruzelski lifted martial law for a month. Presumably we confirmed his worst fears about Western decadent influence on his nation's youth, as a week after we landed back in London he reimposed it again.

By 1984, the Subs had got stale and I felt we were just going through the motions. For me, it became Punk cabaret. I left the band that year and turned my mind to new adventures. After travelling through India, China and other parts of Asia, I flew to America in search of the rock 'n' roll dream, and made it my home for five years.

It was during that time that the events in this book took place. A world tour with Iggy Pop. Seven months of taking Iggy's unique brand of music and performance to just about every major town and city across six continents.

There have been other books written about the phenomenon known as Iggy Pop. Biographies. Facts, figures, how and when. This story has a different agenda. *Neighbourhood Threat* aims to capture and reveal Iggy in his most natural, volatile and exciting environment – the world stage.

This ain't no kiss and tell diary. This is how it was. An eyewitness account of one of the greatest performers in rock music by a member of his touring band. Two hundred and thirty days and nights of ups, downs, triumphs and adversities. A roller-coaster ride… It's gonna be a wild trip!

COLLINS & TAYLOR MANAGEMENT

1619 BROADWAY
SUITE 402
NEW YORK, N.Y. 10019
(212) 265-3740

Mr. Alvin Gibbs
423 1/2 Cloverdale Avenue
Los Angeles, California 90036

E-Mail - TAYLOR.B-US
Telex - 4900008655 CAT-UI

June 24, 1988

Dear Alvin,

Enclosed please find an agreement for your services with the Iggy Pop band for the rehearsals and tour commencing July 8, 1988.

We would appreciate it if you would review, sign and return it to us as soon as possible.

Thank you very much.

Sincerely,

Art Collins/Barry Taylor

7

SOME RAW POWER

Iggy is bearing his soul to a room full of strangers while I stand transfixed at his shoulders. Hunched over a bass guitar, my hands move to hit the notes but my eyes are firmly on the force of nature to the left. For tonight, Iggy is turning this sweating, pulsating den of iniquity into a cathedral. A place of worship. I see it out there in their eyes. As he tears at his flesh, torso wet with perspiration, their eyes say, "We are yours. We have abandoned the mundane, formal world and have reached a collective state of transformation. Take us, lead us. Through the unleashed raw power of your music let us glimpse that hidden place where gods reside. Through the down and dirty rock 'n' roll experience – penetration, elevation, supplication."

Iggy doesn't disappoint; he's the shaman alright. Seeing visions, sharing them, demanding to be believed.

There's a moment under the spotlight when his face turns to mine and he goes into a slow motion spasm. His eyes are on me, but his head is rolling around out of control atop his neck while his body shakes convulsed by what looks like thousands of volts of wild electricity coursing through his taut muscles. Suddenly he leaps up onto the guitarist's Marshall stack and embraces it like a lover. Arms wrapped around the cabinet, face pushed into the speaker, seeking the source and wanting more. Putting the microphone to his lips he howls, "You're the one I love," the gut wrenching declaration in the final chorus of 'Joanna', and proceeds to fuck the amplifier. Crotch pushed in deep, rockin' to and fro while the band provides the loud, naked, dirty rhythm.

It's pure sex. Sex without boundaries. Predatory, animal, instinctual. Sexual power/rock power as one, joined at the hip. Iggy is both shaman and seducer. It's fascinating. For the first time I'm up close, real close, as witness to this phenomenon. My mind's racing, trying to concentrate on the work at hand but, spellbound, I cannot shift my gaze from the performance beside me. For a brief moment I escape back into the eyes, only to feel a vice-like grip around my arms leaving me unable to move. Turning my head to one

side I see Iggy's face next to mine, his chin resting on my shoulder. He has jumped up on my back, arms clamped tight around mine, screaming, "Play, play, play, you rock 'n' roll fucker!"

We are into the final song of the set; as the drummer crashes around his kit bringing the music to a chaotic end, I am unable to play a solitary note, being literally imprisoned in the arms of Iggy. I plead, "Jim, I can't play," but he's not hearing me. Iggy has reached a different plane to the one I inhabit. He keeps yelling, "Play you rock 'n 'roll fucker play!" But I can't move, I can't play.

Then I realise. Then I understand.

He's not exhorting me to play in any conventional sense. Not notes or riffs or structure.

No, he wants me to PLAY!

To explode... To join him in the sublime madness of the moment. Together we tumble to the ground, the bass releasing a deep resonant growl as it collides with the stage floor. Iggy's grinning over me, making sounds like a dog, like a crazy, rabid dog. I get to my feet raising the guitar over my head, letting the low, vibrating feedback grow before bringing the instrument crashing down onto my thighs. A sound like a bomb detonating explodes through the room. Iggy screams, "YES!!"

KILL CITY RENDEZVOUS

I'm living in kill city
Where the debris meets the sea
It's a playground for the rich
But it's a loaded gun to me
'KILL CITY' (Pop/Williamson)

Kill City is Los Angeles. The debris is the human debris of America, the best and the bad drawn across the nation in pursuit of a dream that ends at its sea. I was drawn south to Kill City in the fall of 1986, having swapped a year of San Francisco for smog, freeway shootings and a rock 'n' roll band. One hot June morning at my Hollywood home, I answered the telephone and heard the voice of Andy McCoy.

Andy had been the lead guitarist, songwriter and liquor-fuelled leader of the influential Scandinavian group Hanoi Rocks. We had first met in the early 80s when Hanoi had been the support act for a UK Subs' European tour. I had found him young, brash and slightly arrogant. Despite this, a friendship grew based on our mutual interest in rock music, heroic drinking and chemical experimentation.

Later on, after I had left London to live in the USA, we lost contact, but I had read of Hanoi's demise and heard the rumours, from visiting British groups, concerning out-of-control egos and heavy drug use. Knowing Andy as I did, this seemed kind of inevitable.

When I was told he was in Los Angeles I had mixed feelings. He was a friend, but I heard so many ugly stories concerning his unscrupulous behaviour since his arrival in Kill City that I was unsure if I wanted to hook up with him again. When an acquaintance warned that Andy was asking after me, I told him on no account to give out my home telephone number. He understood all too well; he had loaned Andy his gold pick-up beauty of a guitar, only to spot it in the window of a Hollywood pawn shop the next day. This was the behaviour of a user and a desperado, and I wanted no dealings with either.

But Andy tracked me down somehow and, as I toyed with the idea of pulling out the phone cable, he made me a proposition, "How would you like to be on a world tour playing bass for Iggy Pop?"

I figured that the drugs had finally destroyed his grip on reality and said something like, "Sure, and while you're at it, fix me up with the Rolling Stones!"

He explained that he had secured the gig as lead guitarist on Iggy's forthcoming Instinct World Tour and had convinced Mr Pop, with his considerable powers of persuasion, that I was the man for the bassist's job.

There was something unusually authentic in his voice and I heard myself giving him my address. Sure enough, some time later I opened the door to find Andy standing there grinning, looking like some wigged-out Puerto Rican pimp, holding an open can containing a pre-mixed whiskey cocktail. It was still only 10am.

Andy hadn't changed much over the years – wide hat, impossibly tight strides tucked into fancy cowboy boots and a self-consciously placed cigarette dangling from the corner of his mouth. He still had the look of an outlaw about him and despite my initial reservations I was actually glad to see him again.

"Come on," he ordered, "we're meeting Iggy in 30 minutes, and I want to drink a beer with you first."

The venue for this meeting was a swanky Hollywood apartment, the home of one of Andy's numerous new LA friends. As we sat on the balcony sipping Coronas in the naked sunlight, a candy apple red sports car glided to a halt below us. Andy suddenly shot out of his chair. "Shit man… that's Jim's car. Quick, get these beer bottles out of here." McCoy's friend went to let Iggy in as we frantically put the beer-drinking evidence into a bin liner and lobbed it out of sight. At the time, I couldn't figure out why such drastic action was necessary.

Iggy Pop stepped onto the balcony looking tanned and blonde. The first thing I noticed about him was the leather-like tautness of his skin, and the incredible muscular definition of his upper chest and stomach, shirtless under his jacket. He seemed to have the faint trace of a limp in one leg – a legacy, I was to discover later, of an old touring injury – and looked to be about five foot six tall and not 'Five Foot One' as the song would have it. He had a confident manner, and exuded an air of wiry toughness and sharp intelligence. The last time I'd seen him was on the television a year or so before, putting on the charm and tearing the roof off the TV studio with a hard-assed rendition of 'Real Wild Child' on the *David Letterman Show*. He had been sporting his *Blah Blah Blah* look then – short black hair and expensive leather coat, kind of designer rock 'n' roll. But this was more a street look of tattered leather jacket, frayed blue jeans and longer, bottle-blond hair. You could see the biker influence of his recent musical collaborator, ex-Sex Pistol, Steve Jones.

He smiled a cool smile, shook my hand, said he was pleased to meet me and that I was to call him Jim.

Jim Osterberg, the teacher's son who left the trailer-parks of Michigan to become Iggy Pop and walk on hands as a Stooge. This, however, was not to be a meeting with Iggy Pop. That pleasure would be reserved for another day. This was to be a meeting with the teacher's son.

We sat around and discussed the pleasures and perils, the fools' gold of Los Angeles. He pointed to his wrap-around gangster-style Ray-Bans and told me, "I never trust people who always keep their shades on, but I'm not sure of this weird LA sunlight, so I'll keep them on if it's alright with you." After positioning himself away from the sun, he grilled me on my musical tastes and experience.

Andy told him I had been listening to his music for many years. Iggy said that would be a plus if we worked together. There were so many questions I wanted to ask the man, but I figured that he was auditioning me so I saved them for another time. We talked about guitars and he seemed curious about the sort of sound I aspired to.

"I use a Gibson Thunderbird through an old Ampeg valve amp for a loud, fat sound," I told him. He smiled and simply added, "Cool." I was relieved that my choice of equipment had met with his approval, as many a gig has been lost by the mention of a favourite instrument and sound that is deemed uncool by a prospective employer.

Iggy looked hard at his watch. By that time, we had talked for about an hour and he was running late for a promotional MTV interview. He said his goodbyes, telling me he'd heard good things about my playing and stagecraft and that he would give me a call.

Iggy asked Andy to accompany him to his car. As they left the balcony together, I found a beer we had missed, hidden behind a table leg. I drank it down, wondering what kind of impression I had made on the man I consider to be the seminal figure of two decades of rock music.

Past images came flooding back. Iggy with his Stooges pouting and mean on the covers of their first two killer Elektra records dressed as hip malchicks with 'wha chew looking at?' expressions.

Of learning to play one of my first bass lines from their debut album, the central riff to '1969' which Iggy told me later was based on the Johnny Cash classic 'I Walk The Line'.

Of catching Iggy on the premiere BBC TV rock show of the 70s, *The Old Grey Whistle Test,* after I'd had one too many beers. Literally pushing my drunken face into the screen to study him and his band as they delivered a blistering version of the nihilistic anthem 'I'm Bored' with what looked like a horse's tail sticking out of Pop's leather-clad ass and a less than subtle make-up job smeared over his 'so what!' face.

I remembered how I had liberated a copy of Iggy's *The Idiot* from a Croydon record store while the cashier was looking the other way, because I was penniless. I've never been one for lifting stuff, even as a reckless teenager, but I just *had* to have it, to hear it that night.

I thought back to the time I had a poster pinned to my bedroom wall at my parents' house, a reproduction of the cover of the *Raw Power* LP, with

Iggy leaning on his mike stand, bare death-white torso, tight silver lamé pants, androgynous lipsticked face looking out of frame at something. Maybe looking for action? For appreciation? For anything?... Whatever that look signified, I so much wanted to acquire it, too.

Of seeing my first Iggy Pop show in London in 1978, and being dumbfounded at the sheer intensity of his performance, his physical courage and abandon. That show helped me to redouble my efforts to become a rock 'n' roll musician. It gave me hope and it gave me courage, too.

Now, I was on the cusp of becoming a part of all that. As Iggy's red sports car roared into the distance along Santa Monica Boulevard, and Andy's footsteps made their way back to the balcony, I realised I wanted *very* badly to get this particular gig.

Andy came back looking pleased. "You're in, man. Jim likes you. Expect a phone call tomorrow." He grabbed the Mexican beer out of my hand and took the last swig. I asked him why we had gone to the trouble of hiding the beer bottles when Iggy had arrived. Andy kind of snarled and answered, "It's politics, man... fucking politics." He lobbed the bottle off the balcony and watched it shatter into 100 pieces on the sun-baked sidewalk below.

Iggy's management called me from their New York offices the next day. They asked for everything except my shoe size. Passport number, residential status, previous convictions, Green Card and Social Security information. Art Collins and Barry Taylor were thorough and conscientious managers; it was their job to make sure no prospective member of the Iggy Pop band would prove a future liability.

I answered all their questions and must have checked out alright, as later that same afternoon they phoned with congratulations on getting the gig. They told me to expect the weekly sum of $1200 along with a per diem payment of $30 once we were on the road. Amazing. Not only was I on for a classic global adventure with the legendary Detroit firebrand, but I was also going to be paid handsomely for the pleasure. I lost all pretence of cool by spending the rest of the afternoon shouting down the phone, "I've got it... I've got the fucking gig," at just about everyone I knew in town, and ran up a $200 bill just ringing round friends and family in England, sharing the good news. What's more, just two days later, Iggy's management called again to say that the weekly wage was upped to $1500. A $300 pay rise without having to play a note!

Over lunch that day, my bassist friend Nick Seymour from the Australian group Crowded House reminded me that music was a feast or famine business. He was right. The previous week I had earned less than my $300 pay rise from five LA club dates with my own band, Broken Glass.

In the evening, Iggy phoned to give me details of what would be our first working situation together. The making of the video of 'Cold Metal', which was to be the initial single release from the new *Instinct* record. Iggy sounded up and enthusiastic. "Yeah, it's cool, we've got Sam Raimi to direct it, are you familiar with his work?"

I loved Raimi's *Evil Dead* movies, but the real thrill for me was to finally be physically part of Iggy's work.

It was a cheap cab ride to the Triangle Stage studios the next morning. This was the place where Mack Sennett's Keystone Cops, Laurel And Hardy and (wait for it) The Three Stooges had made their films during Hollywood's golden era. Now it was time for this historic studio to host some rock 'n' roll.

Raimi's stage set was pure rock theatre. Twisting pieces of metal and slabs of neon-lit concrete creating a surreal industrial landscape for Iggy to dance on like some crazed Nijinsky. As Iggy kicked up sand in his solo shots I was introduced to the rest of my fellow passengers in the band.

Paul Garisto had done time with the Psychedelic Furs and provided the drums for the *Instinct* record. He was a New Yorker and his favourite phrase seemed to be, "Fuck this shit," which he used a lot, especially when Raimi placed us precariously on a 20 foot high piece of set that began shaking like milk whenever Paul powered into his drum kit.

Seamus Beaghen was a hairless Londoner who had played with Madness. His would be a dual role of rhythm guitarist and keyboard player.

Steve Jones rode in on an inevitable Harley Davidson motorcycle. An ex-alcoholic and Sex Pistol, Steve had played on the new record but was not to be a full member of the band. He appeared in the video with us, turned up to just a couple of rehearsals, and would play the encore numbers on selected dates of the first American tour only.

Iggy's Japanese wife Suchi sat in the dressing room. I think I may have insulted her by accidentally calling her Sushi a couple of times (bad with names!). She was pretty and seemed shy, so I made a point of chatting to her during a break in filming.

The video shoot went well. Andy and Steve made good shapes both sides of Iggy's hard-assed shoulders, while Paul, Seamus and myself tried to look cool and maintain our balance on the set above them. We worked way into the night, the cameraman filming the action from various angles with Iggy consistent in his high energy performance. Raimi seemed happy with the results and, after drinks on the set for band and crew, we called it a day.

On the journey home the week's events hit me. In seven days, I'd gone from local outfit, local stage to working with my musical idol on a beckoning world stage. It was like a fast car accelerating from 0 to 100mph leaving you unsure if you liked the sensation or not. A bewildering, electrifying state of affairs.

Rehearsals started in earnest on 14 June 1988 at a Santa Monica Boulevard studio. I had been given a list of 35 songs to work on and felt confident with about 25 of them. Iggy arrived at 4pm sharp looking fit and ready to work. For a brief moment I let the fear creep in. Iggy Pop had collaborated with some of the best musicians in rock music – David Bowie, Carlos Alomar, Klaus Kruger, James Williamson, the Sales Brothers and many more. Could I compete? Maybe he wouldn't dig my basslines, and who was I to mess with his music anyway? For the first time I had doubts about my ability to do a good job.

So this is what happens when you get to play with your heroes.

Then I remembered the old martial art axiom, 'the real enemy is within, not without', and reversed gears. All lingering traces of self-doubt evaporated when, on Iggy's command, the band exploded into a predatory rendition of 'Shake Appeal', during which he looked back from his microphone at us and smiled. I knew then that this was going to work out. I knew then that this was going to be fun.

The first set of rehearsals went smoothly. Iggy would bring a list of three or four songs he wanted to concentrate on that day. That was followed by a run-through of the material from the previous rehearsal. At first, we stuck mainly to material from the new *Instinct* album but, later, we worked on more familiar songs from past records such as *The Idiot, Lust For Life, New Values* and *Blah Blah Blah*.

After a rehearsal one night, we all went to the El Cid Spanish restaurant on the edge of town to watch Flamenco dancing, eat paella and drink margaritas. The dancers moved with grace and passion. Iggy loved it. He incorporated some of the Flamenco-style steps he had seen into his dancing. He was becoming more and more movement-orientated with each successive rehearsal.

Andy had been on a drug rehabilitation programme and had surprised me with his professionalism and general togetherness. Unfortunately, it didn't last. He seemed to have traded in drug addiction for alcohol and was beginning to arrive boozed-up, late and unfocused. His playing had become erratic and Iggy was definitely keeping a watchful eye on him. Iggy's own days of habitual drug use and heavy drinking were long over. It had been stressed that this was to be a clean tour, with no drink or soft drugs before rehearsals or performances, and hard drugs forbidden at all times.

This was confirmation of the new, improved Iggy I had read about in recent articles and press interviews. No longer wishing to punish body, mind, and career prospects with liquor and drugs, since his important move to A&M Records in 1986, he had taken to moderation in his pleasures. It was, therefore, an essential part of maintaining Iggy's newly found music biz credibility for him to work with musicians who would be sharp and sober at show-times, who would not bring in temptations that might lead to Iggy taking an unscheduled detour from the hard-won straight and narrow. In light of all this, it is hard to understand why Iggy had even considered Andy McCoy, with his reputation for hedonistic excess, for his touring band in the first place.

Things reached a climax when Andy strolled in one day, three hours late, with the unmistakable smell of hard liquor on his breath. Iggy exploded. "You little fucker, if you mess me around I'm going to fuck you up real good."

Andy muttered something about a traffic jam being responsible for his bad timekeeping, but Iggy wasn't having any of that. "No drinking before rehearsals, you know the rules. Either get your shit together or you're out."

With that he launched the mike stand through the drum kit, kicked over a Marshall amplifier and stormed out of the room 'til his rage had subsided and he was ready to get back to playing some music again.

This worked. Andy arrived at a reasonable time and played consistent guitar for the remainder of the rehearsals. As a result, we saw an increase in the amount of work we could get through in a day.

As the days passed, the set started to take shape. We shifted into third gear; we played the back catalogue of Iggy's material and added some tough Stooges classics to our repertoire. People started to turn up at the rehearsal rooms to listen. Iggy's magician friends from New York, Penn & Teller, came by to wish us well and requested that we play 'Search And Destroy' for them. We obliged.

A jewellery maker and Merlin look-alike named Axil brought over rings and bracelets as gifts for the band, and danced with joyous abandon with his girlfriend at the back of the room as we pumped out the music and Iggy found his voice.

An LA rich boy, whose father owned a sporting goods company, dropped by to give Iggy some golf clubs, having read that Iggy was a fan of the sport. He was followed by the film actor James Russo, a mutual friend of both Iggy's and mine.

Some days, there was such a variety of people in that room that I began to feel like a musical extra in a Fellini movie. However, it did provide us with an audience of sorts and as such, slowly warmed us up to the idea of performing.

On a day off Iggy turned up at my apartment wearing some new shades and a white cap bearing the legend, 'PINKS HOTDOGS THE BEST IN THE WORLD', which he had purchased after sampling a chilli-dog at that renowned LA establishment. We spent that hot Californian afternoon together looking for shoes. As we drove around from store to store, I asked him about his family background and the talk turned to marriage, and the advantages of a steady home life. Over a delicious Sashimi and green tea lunch at a Venice Beach Japanese restaurant, I asked him how he had met his wife Suchi.

"I did a show in Tokyo," he explained. "Saw her in the crowd from up on the stage and something just clicked, so I asked one of the road crew to invite her to the dressing room to talk, and we got on so well that we've been together ever since."

The roadie in question later told me that Iggy had simply instructed him after the show to bring the Japanese girl in the glasses backstage. Having gone out into the auditorium, he noted at least a dozen optically-challenged daughters of the Rising Sun standing around. Not having a clue which one Iggy meant, he opted for the closest – Suchi. Whether she was in fact the woman that Iggy had clicked with from up on the stage, he, nor we, shall never know.

The next day Iggy picked me up in the red convertible for the first of three final rehearsals. At the studio we found our newly arrived British road crew and sound engineer busily stencilling the equipment with the 'IGGY POP INSTINCT' logo and placing amps and other pieces of back-line into protective flight-cases for the tour ahead. Henry McGroggan, our short,

Scottish, no-nonsense tour manager (TM) handed us each a copy of an itinerary containing the dates and information for the initial 'small clubs' warm-up tour of the USA. The excitement and nerves were building with the realisation that we were now just days away from playing in front of a paying crowd. Andy rustled up some feedback on his Gibson guitar and we tore through the set – 'Instinct', 'Kill City', 'High on You', '1969', 'Power and Freedom', 'Tough Baby', 'Passenger', 'No Fun', 'Cold Metal', 'Square Head', 'I Feel Alright', 'Shake Appeal', 'Penetration', 'Five Foot One', 'Weird Sin', 'Joanna', 'Beyond the Law', 'Cry for Love', 'Winners and Losers', 'Search and Destroy', and 'Your Pretty Face Is Going to Hell'. The designated encore numbers were 'Easyrider', 'I Wanna Be Your Dog' and 'I Gotta Right'. This list was to be our basic blueprint for the months to come. A solid structure on which to add or subtract as the world tour progressed.

During a break from rehearsing, Iggy told me a story set in LA in the early 1970s. A time when his capacity for drugs, sleazy sex and booze was legendary. He'd been up all night at his Hollywood apartment popping pills. Uppers followed by downers, in a vain attempt to achieve some kind of chemical balancing act. The sun was coming up and, feeling hungry, Iggy grabbed a couple of beefburgers out of the ice box and turned on the gas for the oven. As he knelt in front of the open oven door with a burger in each hand he suddenly realised he needed matches to light the gas. At that moment Iggy experienced a complete and alarming physical seizure.

"I couldn't move a muscle," he explained. "Couldn't speak, couldn't do anything but kneel there breathing in the gas with the meat slowly thawing in each hand."

Although he couldn't move, he could think, and the ramifications of the situation were obvious to him. In a short while he would be overcome by the

gas. His head would fall into the oven and, some time later, they would find his lifeless body and conclude that he had committed suicide. As Iggy resigned himself to becoming another rock 'n' roll casualty the next door neighbours smelt escaping gas and came to the rescue.

"They kicked down the door and dragged me outta there."

"Shit," I said, "what a close call."

"Yeah," he agreed, "but if I had died and they figured it was suicide, what the fuck would they have made of the beefburgers?"

What indeed? Maybe a final comment on the futility of existence, or a bizarre offering to the gods? Either way, Iggy was sure a lot of people would have read some mystic significance into what was just meant to be breakfast.

By the final rehearsal, we were sounding like a band. A little shaky in places, but a hard driving rock 'n' roll band none the less. While the rest of us had worked on building a solid music muscle, Iggy had slowly pushed his voice and loosened up his lithe body for the gruelling months ahead. On the last run-through of the set, his voice sounded strong as he contorted himself into those impossible shapes and poses so familiar from those early photographs of him performing with the Stooges. During 'Weird Sin', he leaned forward and raised his leg over his back so that his heel touched his shoulder and just swayed there; he defied gravity for a while before twisting himself into another reptilian shape. He got down on all fours, pushed his face and chest towards the ceiling and barked at the moon for 'Now I Wanna Be Your Dog'. It was fascinating to watch the way the understated and steady Jim Osterberg was slowly, day-by-day, being replaced, or rather complemented, by his wild alter-ego, Iggy Pop.

Over these rehearsal weeks I had learnt some more about how Iggy/Jim operated on both a professional and personal level. As a professional, he seemed totally focused on the work in progress. Preparing for the world tour meant him having to forego parties, clubbing and late nights out drinking with the band, *and* non-participation in the endless pleasures the city of fallen angels had to offer.

After all, Iggy was 41 years old and had discovered in recent times that it was necessary to work harder and harder to maintain his vocal ability and physical shape. After a day's rehearsing, he would drive back to his Hollywood hotel for an evening with Suchi, to rest up, work out material for the next day session, do an occasional interview and take care of business. He had cut out cigarette smoking completely to preserve his voice, and continually practised singing exercises to keep it strong and extend its range.

There was one particular afternoon when I hitched a ride home in Iggy's convertible. He pushed a cassette into the car player saying, "Don't mind me... I need to loosen up my throat a little," and started following the voice exercises on the tape at full volume. It was a glorious LA day and the red racer's top was down, which was fine when we growled and rumbled at top speed along the boulevards, but got a touch embarrassing when we had to come to a halt at a stop light. Motorists either side of us would suddenly be confronted by the bizarre apparition of Iggy with his weird insect eye sunglasses and peroxide Medusa hair yelling out the escalating notes along with the cassette at ear shattering volume. A couple of 'who's your crazy friend' looks came my way, but most laughed while I shot back a weak smile, shrugged my shoulders and slid further and further down my seat 'til the green light appeared and the virile engine's roar once again provided the audio camouflage to Iggy's vocal gymnastics. Iggy really didn't give a shit what those motorists thought. I don't think he even noticed them. He had work to do, a mission that was a source of pride, so he continued his voice training at top volume right up to delivering me to my doorstep, and no doubt all the way through the city to his.

As well as training and keeping his voice in shape, Iggy also worked hard at maintaining his incredible muscular physique. Up at six each morning he would spend a full hour doing exercises and stretches before taking breakfast with his wife. It was apparent that the watch word for the new Ig was 'discipline'. Something I had not anticipated.

On a personal level his relationship with the other members of the band and myself was – apart from that one forceful, "Get your shit together," warning for Andy – one of seeming respect and camaraderie. He encouraged our views on his choice of songs and our input on arrangements or improvements to material. Iggy was not precious about his music at all. Andy came up with a bunch of new arrangements for his songs. Iggy enthusiastically acknowledged the improvements these made to them and encouraged McCoy to work on more. I played around with a new beginning for 'Five Foot One' with drummer Paul; Iggy looked up from his cup of coffee and said, "Hey, that's great, I've never done it that way before. Let's keep that!"

It was also becoming apparent to me how bright and educated – in the true sense of that word – Iggy was. He was very well read and had a seemingly encyclopaedic mind when it came to geography, art, history or just general knowledge. Occasionally I'd bring a *Time* magazine or a *LA Times* with me to glance through during our rehearsal lunch break. On raising a current issue of politics or foreign affairs, Iggy would inevitably jump into the conversation and surprise us all with his command of the relevant facts and figures and his articulate, informed insights. This was also something I had not anticipated.

During this stage of the game, at least, Iggy came across as a well-balanced, intelligent, career-driven individual. But hey... these were still early days!

With the final rehearsal accomplished there was nothing more to be done but drive home and mentally prepare for the tour ahead. For those of you who have not tried it, the act of offering yourself to an unknown and expectant audience is akin to performing psychological Hari Kiri. Up on that stage, you are exposed and vulnerable; to create the necessary illusion of confidence and ease requires not just musical but mental preparation. Of course the heaviest burden for this lay on Iggy's shoulders but, as his band, we carried the responsibility to provide a musical and visual backdrop worthy of his performance and reputation.

The next day I played over the set on my own, cutting out any superfluous runs and unnecessary flourishes in my bass playing. Satisfied, I picked up the tour itinerary and turned to page one. There in bold type was the first show of the Instinct World Tour. It read "Friday 8 July 1988 – The Whisky-A-Go-Go, Los Angeles, California."

It would seem the first neighbourhood under threat would be my own.

PACIFIC CONCERTS PRESENTS

IGGY POP

AND

BY SPECIAL REQUEST

SoCiAL-DiSToRTioN

106.7 KROQ HIT

TO PERFORM THEIR #1 "PRISON BOUND"

SOLID CUT

JULY 8

8:00 P.M.

AT THE

WHISKY-A-GO-GO

8901 SUNSET STRIP, HOLLYWOOD, CA.

ART BY
SUPERBIGBUCKS PRODUCTIONS
PRINTED BY UNCLE CAL

Tickets available at TICKETMASTER including May Co., Music Plus and Sportmart Stores and the UCLA Central Ticket Office. To charge by phone call (713) 480-3232 or (714) 740-2000 or Chargeline (213) 688-7380

22

NIGHTCLUBBING

The Whisky-A-Go-Go is pretty much a legendary venue in rock 'n' roll circles. Jim Morrison and The Doors used its stage to refine their particular brand of musical poetry, and just about every name rock performer of the 60s and 70s had either played there, or had partaken at some time of its hedonistic delights.

That sultry Los Angeles night, The Whisky's marquee announced, in two foot high red plastic letters, that it was the turn of the Iggy Pop Band.

Earlier, the soundcheck had gone well. No hitches with the equipment, and the selection of songs we had compiled into a set sounded tough and tight.

Steve Jones joined us with his low-slung Les Paul for a couple. He was to come out to play for the encore section only, but even so, confided in me that he was pretty nervous about the prospect.

"Ain't you nervous about the gig tonight?" he asked Paul, who sat impassive behind his drums.

"Nah, why should I be?" Paul replied.

Steve persisted, "Alvin are you nervous?"

"Yeah, I'm plenty nervous," I said. This made Steve feel better.

"Good lad, you wouldn't be human unless you felt a bit nervous. Paul Garisto you're a bleedin' liar... I bet you're as nervous as the rest of us, you New York bullshitter!"

Nobody asked Iggy how his nerves were holding up. It was obvious. Though this was just the first in a series of small club warm-up dates, we knew that he was aware that every Los Angeleno A & R man, music biz suit, critic, poser and swinging dick would be at our show tonight. Eyes, ears and busy mouths; if Iggy failed to satisfy them and the Whisky crowd, they were ready and able to pass on the word that the gold of his talent had finally turned to base metal.

"Yeah man, Iggy's lost it... he's too old, can't hack it any more... that last band he had was so... so... SO much better."

You get the picture.

It's like that for him each time a new record is released and a promotional tour follows. He becomes a tightrope walker, balancing on a high, slender

wire with the crowd watching from below, waiting for a fall.

On my arrival, there was a line of hopefuls stretching from the main entrance right around the block. No chance. The Whisky's official capacity is 450, and I was told these tickets had been snapped up within an hour of going on sale a couple of days before.

Inside, the atmosphere was electric, with a tangible air of expectation filling the packed and sweltering room.

The moment of truth was at hand.

As I walked into the dressing room, Iggy gave me a friendly wave and a warm hello, and I saw that even though the pressure was on, he was holding up well. Andy, Paul, Seamus and Steve were already there standing around, dressed for stage, looking not unlike four solemn grooms waiting to walk down the aisle for a shotgun wedding.

I needed a beer and despite the pre-gig ban on booze I figured one wouldn't matter any, so I pulled out an ice-cold Coors from the cooler and started drinking. Nothing was said, and having set a precedent, Andy and Paul felt safe to casually follow my example and grab themselves a can each. It helped ease the fear.

Mark Edwards the guitartek, Jos Grain the drumtek (no-one's a roadie any more, they're all goddamn teks nowadays) and Tim Sunderland our sound engineer, came in one after the other to tell us everything was ready and to bid us good luck.

The house lights went off, with our intro tape of rhythmic African drums and chanting coming on LOUD over the Whisky's PA, increasing the excitement and building tension, both in the audience and backstage.

Iggy had taken off his glasses in a kind of a Clark Kent scenario and was winding up for the hour and a half ahead, windmilling his arms, flexing his muscles, gathering up that rock power until the metamorphosis from Osterberg to Iggy was complete.

Henry opened the dressing room door holding a torch. "Time to do the business," he told us, and following behind Monsieur Pop, we stepped out onto the torch-lit stairway that led to the stage. This is the moment. The drug. So intense, electrifying and fearful. Words can't do justice to that mixed bag of emotions, to the sensation that attacks the spine as you take to the stage and the crowd acknowledge your presence with a roar of approval.

As we stepped onto the Whisky stage, Iggy grabbed the mike stand and strutted to the edge to address the mix of rockbiz, musicologists and sensualists. He screamed, "Hello, you motherfuckers!" As the crowd roared their own communal greeting back, Paul's drum-count came to an end and the band kicked into a high octane version of the title track from the new record, *Instinct*.

From song one, Iggy decided to take the room by using sheer force. Grabbing out at each one of them; confronting, demanding and receiving respect. He was a raging bull. The Jake La Motta of rock 'n' roll. Iggy had them in the palm of his sweaty hand, as he danced and careered about the stage to the delight of the increasingly vocal crowd. We knew this was The Real Deal and things were going our way.

By the encores, with Steve Jones joining us to play some hard driving guitar on 'I Wanna Be Your Dog', the room was as one in its adoration.

Sweating and smiling after the last note, we headed back to the dressing room in the knowledge that Iggy's reputation had been sustained, if not enhanced, and the word would go out that this night, at least, rock 'n' roll did not take a dive.

Backstage, our room quickly filled up with well-wishers, management, invited musicians and back slapping record company types, all eager to show their appreciation by sharing our champagne and sampling our food. Singer Ian Astbury and guitarist Billy from those fine purveyors of post-Led Zeppelin metallic riffing, The Cult stepped over to congratulate me on a job well done. I spied a couple of my punk rock heroes, Joey and Johnny of that classic New York quartet, The Ramones, sharing a Budweiser with Iggy.

Eric, Iggy's teenage son, turned up looking just like his father did back in 1968, except somewhat taller. Long, straight, brown hair, boyish good looks, snake hipped and pencil thin.

Eric was born out of wedlock in 1970 and had been raised by his mother, Paulette Benson, in Los Angeles with Iggy staying in contact with his son during breaks in his touring and recording schedules. During his visits, he had forged a close and affectionate relationship with Eric. After Paulette started to have serious difficulties with the boy in the mid 80s, Iggy took responsibility for his son's welfare and financial needs. Eric still lived in LA, and Iggy had told me he was proud that his son had got himself a regular day-job, working a 40 hour week at a Melrose Avenue clothing store, and was now able to support himself.

Backstage that night, it quickly became obvious that Eric had misjudged his alcohol intake as he staggered around the room, stumbling into people and knocking the wine over. I made a grab for him and got him to sit down. Must be tough for him to deal with a situation like this, I thought. Must be tough having a father who casts such a big shadow.

Iggy came over, concerned, to check out his boy. He got drumtek Joss to go down to the street to get him a cab, so he would be sure Eric got home safely to sleep it off.

There were no plans for a post-show dinner, or extended celebration, as Iggy needed to get some rest for our following day's show. So, shortly after Eric left, I stepped out of the Whisky's exit and hailed down a cab.

Outside on the Sunset Boulevard sidewalk, there were a bunch of boozed-up casualties from the show, lurching around with bottles of cheap wine. One of them recognised me as a member of the Iggy Pop band, and came over and kind of swayed in front of me, before getting out the words, "Man… you were great tonight. Iggy was so cool, and you guys fuckin' rocked, man!"

"Thanks," I said, getting into the cab. I felt good about the way things had gone.

Back home I shared my feelings with my wife. "Don't forget," she said "you still have over 200 nights to come."

She had a point.

I opened my door the next morning to yet another platinum LA day. It was also the day of another gig in town by the sonic architect and his new band, this time downtown at the Scream Club, a big cavernous venue opposite MacArthur Park.

Our second soundcheck of the week went smoothly, with first night nerves ditched, and after our successful Whisky performance, morale high.

Show-time. Two thousand Iggites digging it, soaking it up, throwing it back with less biz in tonight and more genuine thrill seekers relishing the Iggy spectacular and yelling their approval. Steve Jones came on for the dessert part of the set again, and played an especially mean solo during 'Easy Rider', working that longhaired biker, macho image for all it's worth. And it's worth quite a lot in a city like LA – at least a one album deal.

After the show, it was elated faces again. Iggy truly seemed relieved and happy. Backstage, I poured him a champagne, and as we clinked glasses with the sweat of the gig still drip, drip, dripping off our steaming bodies, he smiled his smile and said, "Thanks man, great show."

That night, there was no going home. The band, with the crew, would be travelling overnight on board a mobile home-style sleeper bus to San Francisco, with Iggy and Suchi spending the night in LA and flying out in the morning. Steve Jones was not due to play with us again until our important New York *New Music Seminar* appearance.

A 405 mile ride to the city by the bay, and Andy, Paul, Seamus and I were still buzzing from our Scream show, with heavy doses of adrenalin pumping round. Very high on rock energy. We had taken all the leftover booze and grass we could find from the dressing room and, as the miles sped by, had ourselves a mobile party until the early hours of the next morning.

The bus was really something. A front section with tables and seats, cooker, couch, TV and tape player, and a huge fridge stocked full of beers, wine and food. The mid-section was for sleeping with bunk beds for 12, complete with bedding and reading lights. In the rear, there was a bathroom and back room – where most of the action took place – with its comfortable crescent moon-shaped couch, wide-screen TV, stereo system and well-appointed bar set-up. I've honestly lived in a lot shabbier forms of accommodation in my time.

As we slept, Southern California became Northern California, and the darkness gave way to light.

Henry woke us up as the bus came to a halt outside the Miyako Hotel in SF's Japan-town. I knew this city well, having lived a year in 'Frisco before going south for professional reasons, and a number of my friends still lived and worked there.

The Miyako, as one would anticipate from its name and location, had a thoroughly Japanese look and feel to it. My room had shoji (wood and paper) screens and doors and a very deep Asian-style bath in which the piping hot water came up to my chin when I sat down.

That evening's show was to take place at the Fillmore Theatre on Geary Street, just five blocks from our hotel. This was another venue that could conjure up rock fantasies. Hippy vibe. Dead-heads, acid and the Summer of Love. Honey-limbed flower child shivas dancing to Jefferson Airplane, fuelled by Timothy Leary's politics of ecstasy. The Fillmore reeked of it.

The San Francisco Fillmore was the house that the legendary promoter Bill Graham built. In the 60s and early 70s, Graham owned and promoted shows at the two most important and prestigious rock venues in the USA: the Fillmore West in SF and the Fillmore East in New York City. During their heyday, these two theatres showcased and secured the fabled careers of the likes of Jimi Hendrix, the Rolling Stones, Otis Redding and Northern California's very own Jefferson Airplane, Santana and the Grateful Dead. They became the happening venues of that era, and Bill Graham secured his place in rock history by running them his way, bringing sadly lacking honesty and integrity to rock 'n' roll promotions and the music biz in general.

A couple of years after my performance with Iggy at the Fillmore, Bill Graham died in a helicopter crash. He will be sorely missed.

Iggy had us work out a new ending for 'Tough Baby' during our 'check. Instead of just a straight stop, we developed a dynamic three-section ending, which felt better and added a new, theatrical dimension to the song.

I had dinner back at the hotel, followed by my established ritual from past tours of bath, shave and a quick nap to relax the nerves and conserve energy before a show. Back on the bus for a quick ride back to Geary Street, and onto the famed Fillmore stage to strut our stuff.

It proved to be a good show. Solid and steady, in contrast to the two LA all-out assaults of the previous nights. I discussed this with Iggy afterwards. We agreed that it was because of the quality of the 'Frisco crowd: bright Berkeley college kids, older literary Allen Ginsberg look-alikes, with a sprinkling of Haight Ashbury hipsters and some beer-fuelled punks. A good mixture of the cerebral and the visual.

Backstage, I introduced Iggy to my brother-in-law who had been a big fan of Iggy's brand of metallic rock 'n' roll for many years. The thing was, I introduced Iggy to my brother-in-law as Jim. As the name passed from my lips, I was almost sure I saw a flicker of annoyance in Iggy's eyes. Yeah, of course… Jim is a name reserved for his work associates, family and friends. I made a mental note not to introduce him to others as Jim again.

Back at the Miyako, Iggy and Suchi sent out an invitation via Henry to join them for supper at a Korean barbecue restaurant across the street. I declined. It would take me a few more shows to get into road shape, and I was pretty tired out from the three shows in a row. I settled for privacy, rest and room-service Japanese delicacies and sake instead.

*

It was a leisurely start the next morning; I even managed breakfast before departing with band and crew in a convoy of cabs for SF airport.

"Ladies and gentlemen, American Airlines are now ready for boarding flight 390 bound for O'Hare Airport, Chicago," came over the airport intercom an hour later. Smooth take-off and a skilled hostess with the perfect bedside manner served the band and crew snacks and cocktails as the coastline of California receded beneath us. I'd copped myself a window seat with Andy beside me to my left. We'd only been in the air an hour and already McCoy was into his seventh Bloody Mary... Still, it was a day off and it is important that a man has his hobbies. We glided into Chicago to a featherbed landing. TM Henry and the crew raced off to organise the luggage and transport, while I desperately tried to help Andy locate a piece of hash he'd lost down the side of his seat at some stage during the journey.

"Man," he said with a tragic voice, pointing underneath his seat, "I know it's got to be somewhere down there, for Chrissakes."

This was cool. Five minutes into the tour, and McCoy was already leaving a trail of illegal substances in his wake. It was an omen of what was to come.

During the long taxi ride to the hotel, Iggy told me how he had moved to Chicago to study the Blues at the tender age of 19. It was the winter of 1966, and he had been a drummer back then.

"I lived in a cold basement room and just about made a living playing the skins with bluesmen in the Chicago south-side clubs for some eight months. After a time, though, I came to realise that only a black man can really play the blues. You see, it drips like honey from their fingertips, it's instinctual. No skinny-assed whiteboy can compete with that, man. My realisation took me back to Michigan and the formation of The Stooges."

The next day, another gig, another dollar. That night, we were earning dinner at Club Metro, a mid-size venue next door to the stadium home of the Chicago baseball team, the Cubs. It was another good un, with an up-for-it crowd, the band trading some cool licks and Iggy moving like liquid fire, leaving the stage to a sea of waving, grasping hands.

After drying off following the encores, I joined the rest of the guys for a few vodkas in the little bar in the basement of the venue. Despite our protestations, Iggy and Suchi declared they were tired and headed back to base, leaving us to party into the wee small hours.

The bar was crowded with punters from our just-finished gig, and the barman told us that our drinks were on the Metro's tab for as long as we wanted them. Music to our ears.

I immediately got down to doing some serious damage to their supplies of Stolichnaya vodka, poured out, looking like syrup, from a bottle kept in a freezer, into shot glasses that Andy and I stacked up one on the other. By the time we had built a tower of 20 or so of those glasses, a couple of Illinois girls with moon pale skin, beaming smiles and what I figured just had to be Wonderbras on, came over to Andy and I to introduce themselves and thank us, "for the wonderful show." Andy immediately

made a play for the blonde; her equally attractive, raven-haired friend grabbed my arm and asked me if I'd like a drink.

"No," I told her. "That's not necessary. What can I get you?" Together we stacked up another 20 or so of those shot glasses, and things got kind of steamy. Andy, who, moments before had been getting it on with his chick in a corner of the club, came over and whispered in my ear that it was time to get them back to the hotel for a full-on orgy in my room.

"My room! What do you mean my room, McCoy?" I asked, drunkenly.

Andy's answer had a unique logic to it. " 'Cos if my wife phones up, I won't be there to answer with some chick yelling around in the background."

I stared at him a second and said, "But I'm married too, as you well know. What if it's my wife who phones?"

Andy just shrugged, and finished off with, "Well, suit yourself man, suit yourself," and went back to investigate the nether regions of his new friend's mouth with his busy tongue.

I looked at the girl who had clung onto me, and an appropriate word jumped into my drunken brain. 'Desirable'. She *was* desirable; a fine long-legged dream of a woman. Then bits of Andy's conversation came back to me. Wife. Phone call... Shit, *I* was married. I was married, and I'd been away from my wife for less than 24 hours, and there I was already contemplating having sex with some stranger in a strange city. That was no good. I got the girl another round of drinks, made my excuses, and headed for the exit.

The next morning, the bad news was that I had no recall of getting back to the hotel, having awoken fully-clothed at the foot of my bed, with a mysterious, half-eaten sandwich in my hand (ham on rye) and the hangover of the century. The good news was that it was another no-gig day, and we were back on The Big Bus, destination Detroit.

In the back room, I kicked back with some black coffee and aspirin and watched the scenery go by. Round Lake Michigan, out of Illinois and into Michigan state. Farms, small timber-house communities, pine trees and livestock. Clean air, country vibe, disrupted occasionally by a giant truck thundering by like some automotive Tyrannosaurus Rex.

I joined driver Jim Boatman up front to escape Seamus's endless James Brown tape in the back room, and settled for Jim's country music cassettes instead, with Crystal Gayle singing her songs of unrequited love.

Now Jim was an interesting sort. A red-bearded, tall, strapping resident of the town of Nashville with a thick Tennessee accent and a pocketful of stories.

"Yep, driven them all at one time or another. Willie Nelson, now, there's a gentleman, but he sure gets some strange-looking women coming to his shows. What's got dyed hair, 200 hairy legs, 200 tattooed arms and no teeth?"

"Don't know, Jim."

"The front row of females at a Willie Nelson show."

"That bad, huh?"

"Yessiree, that bad!" said Mr Boatman.

Jim was not exactly New Man material. By the time Lake Erie

came into view, we were into the home straight for Detroit and Jim had got to his Julio Iglesias recollections.

"He sure can pull some stylish pussy, boy; model-types, with money an' all… he had to fight them off. Caused me some grief one day, though."

"What happened?" I asked.

"Julio goes and does himself a turd about so long, in the toilet back there!" Jim continued, taking his hands off the wheel for a second, and placing them about two feet apart, before wrestling back control of the bus again.

Now I've heard of fishermen telling tall tales, but this is too much…

"Blocked up the entire system, boy, had to pull the bus over, and take me a stick to that big shit, fish it out and bury it at the side of the road. Julio put it down to the king-sized steak he had eaten the night before, so I says to him, 'Julio', I says, 'from now on, you're on goddamn vegetables and rice… another shit like that and I quit!' "

Julio Iglesias, purveyor of cool, Latino charm and bus-busting turds… Nice story.

He continued in this vein right up to our arrival on the forecourt of the Omni Hotel in the heart of Detroit, our home for the next couple of days. Again, Iggy and Suchi had not ridden in with us. They would fly in from Chicago later that evening.

After getting my keys from the desk clerk, I made straight for my room, put the 'Do Not Disturb' sign on my door and spent a quiet evening in, reading the first batch of newspaper Iggy Pop band concert reviews that were waiting for us at reception, courtesy of Iggy's management team, Collins And Taylor. All were good, with especially enthusiastic lines in the *Hollywood Reporter* and *Chicago Tribune*… Well, that was a relief.

Next day's gig was a real bastard. Detroit, of course, is Iggy's home territory, so one would think a Hail The Hometown Hero scenario would have been on the cards. No such thing. Faces with, 'Impress me,' written all over them, flying beer cans and a general 'Fuck you' attitude prevailed for the first half of the show. Iggy stalked the stage, screaming hate and retribution, before swinging them round song by song, working double hard and winning an enthusiastic encore. It was tough work, but Iggy is a tough motherfucker.

Prior to getting on Jim's bus the next day, with Iggy and Suchi finally joining us for Big Bus Fun, I picked up a copy of Hunter S. Thompson's *Generation Of Swine,* and a diary from the Omni newsagents. Now I could keep a day-to-day account of my touring experiences; who knows, I might even write a book about them some time, and my powers of recall are not always so great.

Here's a sample of my handy-work…

Friday 15 July – Cleveland
Staying at the Stouffers Hotel, a big, rambling train station of a place. Makes Waterloo look inviting and intimate. Temperature's rising. Hot day, and sticky evening's work at the 1100 seater Phantasy Theatre. No frills, and somewhat satisfying. A McDonald's hamburger of a gig.

Saturday 16 July – Washington DC
Fuck it's hot! A 110° day, with humidity to match. Thank Christ the bus has industrial-strength air conditioning. A 369 mile drive to America's capital and a night off to do a little midnight rambling.

Sunday 17 July – Washington DC
Quick sortie to check out the sights. White House, etc, with Iggy missing out due to a knee injury acquired on the drum riser in Cleveland. Didn't stop him none at the gig, though. Muscles and guts. The 9.30 Club is the venue for one of the finest gigs I ever played with the UK Subs, and again, they don't disappoint. Packed to the rafters, ultra-hot and sweaty. Crowd goes ape-shit. Killer show.

Monday 18 July – Philadelphia
City of brotherly love, home of Rocky, and location of this evening's soirée. Best part of tonight was the unbelievable chicken liver spaghetti I bought Iggy, Suchi and Andy at an all-night diner, post performance… That kind of night.

Tuesday 19 July – Boston
Venue's the Channel, and the show is going out live on Boston radio. Soundcheck gives us cause for concern (very odd sounding room) and when we take to the stage for the real thing, it becomes a waking nightmare. Bass cuts out twice, and the overall sound is awful. Iggy threatens to crush the house monitor man's skull in with his mike stand unless things improve (which they didn't) and I screw up the changes in 'Winners and Losers' and the intro to 'Search and Destroy' big time. Much wailing and gnashing of teeth after.

On the next day's bus drive to New York, Iggy decides to do the brave thing and puts on the Boston radio tape, to cries of, "No, for fuck's sake, anything but that!" from me and similar expressions of terror from others in the band. Surprisingly, it was not nearly as bad as we had anticipated, which is just as well, as it was released the following year as a live album, imaginatively titled, *Iggy Pop – Live at the Channel.*

NY City's Mayflower Hotel is situated on Central Park West, on the money side of the divine island of Manhattan. After the drive from Boston, I'd wanted to relax in its well-stocked bar to drink a couple of margaritas, or perhaps stretch out on my king-sized hotel bed and catch a nap before the night's action. Instead, I had barely enough time to put my suitcase down, before I was hustled out by tour manager Henry to the Ritz for that inconvenient but necessary rock 'n' roll tradition, the soundcheck.

That night's show was very important. It was the climax of the *New Music Seminar* – an annual, week-long convention where A & R sorts, managers, record execs and the men/women who represent the Music Biz get to network, make deals, trade information and most importantly, tear the ass out of their business expense accounts with spouses, girl/boyfriends and mistresses/toy boys and in some notable cases, all three. In other words, another high-wire walk of a gig, minus safety net.

Just enough time after our 'check to shower and pick out some threads back at the Mayflower.

My clothes were starting to smell of stale sweat and laundry neglect, but I eventually found a jeans-shirt-jacket combination, with an acceptable odour, which I placed into a carry-all, referred to by all touring musicians as a 'gig bag'.

This kind of rotting, stinking wardrobe problem is a common occurrence on the road. A lot of sweat is expended during the course of a show, and generally, musicians just fling their perspiration-soaked garments back into their suitcases without a thought, back at the hotel. Of course, we fully intend to get them dry-cleaned and laundered at some stage in the near future, but being lazy fuckers as a breed, somehow we never get round to it until mould is visible, and the foul stench coming from the case is enough to overpower even the most hardy customs official.

Back at the Ritz, Iggy was anxiously pacing the dressing room. "Where is that little fucker…? Henry, go find him."

Andy's gone missing. Somewhere between the Mayflower and the Ritz, McCoy and his cab had disappeared, and with five minutes to go to showtime, it was not looking good. Seamus reckoned he saw Andy get into a cab back at the hotel with some black girl, and had assumed they were heading straight here.

Panic.

The minutes passed. Iggy looked like he was ready to kill, while various crew members ran up and down East 11th Street in the hope of finding our AWOL lead guitarist. Just as the situation reached its critical mass, Andy strolled into the room, calmly poured himself a wine and made himself comfortable on the dressing room couch. He looked up at our incredulous faces.

"Oh right, yeah, sorry. Had a few problems getting here... not late, am I?"

There was no time for anger, for questions or answers. The intro tape was on, and it was time to go down to the stage. As we made our way from the dressing room, Andy pulled me to one side.

"Man, I'm really out of it"

"What are you talking about?" I asked.

He continued, "Some black chick I met at the hotel said her place was round the corner from here and we should stop by for a quick joint on the way."

"Yeah, so...? I've seen you smoke joints like most people smoke Marlboro Lights."

"That's true, but the thing was, after we smoked it, she told me the grass was laced with PCP."

"PCP... what, you mean Angel Dust?"

"Yeah, fuckin' Angel Dust man, and it's kicked in like a mother."

He was visibly shaken, and the look in his eyes read, 'Help; I'm out of my depth here, I think I'm about to blow it.'

For the past couple of weeks, I'd been half-expecting Andy to go pharmaceutical. Now, seconds before we were about to go on and play the most important show of the USA club tour, in front of a house full of critics, muzos and rock biz, he was in the grip of a mind-scrambling episode, courtesy of one of the most obnoxious drugs known to man or beast. PCP, or phencyclidine hydrochloride as it is chemically known, was originally designed as a drug for knocking out horses and other large animals. Andy was not a particularly large animal, but he did have a rather unique sense of timing. I was almost lost for words, but not quite...

"Oh shit... okay, just try and hold it together... try to focus on the music. Get Jos to give you loads of orange juice; the vitamin C will help. Run around a lot, sweat some of that chemical out of your body."

Too late for more advice. Iggy had bounded out onto the stage, and Henry's voice boomed out, "Hurry up, you twos, you're on."

As I collected my Thunderbird from the guitartek, I glanced at Andy, saw the panic in his face, and said a silent prayer to the benevolent gods of rock 'n' roll.

ZOMBIE MOTHERFUCKERS

Thirty seven thousand feet. A business class seat on a Pan American 747 winging its way south to Brazil. Exotic expectations and a buzz steadily growing with each passing hour and each stewardess-delivered vodka-tonic.

Across the aisle sat Iggy, reading. He was deep in concentration, lost in the pages of one of Carlos Castaneda's many mystic volumes. Asleep, her delicate head resting on his shoulder, Suchi was to his right. Directly in front, Seamus listened to a tape on his Walkman; probably James Brown. Paul and Andy sat ahead, ambushing another harassed member of the flight crew for more booze.

Yes, Andy was still with us. It was a close run thing at that Ritz show, though. Despite my visions of a humiliating gig featuring an out of control, tripping guitarist, foaming at the mouth, high on Angel Dust, Andy somehow got it together to pull off a job-saving if sometimes surreal performance. He heeded my advice to run around and sweat it out by duck walking, running on the spot and looking at times more like an insane aerobics instructor than a rock 'n' roll guitarist. But it helped. By the end of the show, the audience at least looked vaguely human to him, as opposed to the frightening neon carpet of savage multicoloured lizard men he'd played to in his first hour on stage.

During the seven days that followed Andy's drugged ciggies episode, the band and crew kicked around NY city with the Mayflower as our base. We played a couple of very low key shows in venues with names such as Toad's Place and Lobster-A-Go-Go, out-of-state small club dates to keep us musically active and work out kinks that had been identified in the set during our previous two weeks on the road.

Iggy made a high profile, if somewhat nervous appearance on the David Letterman talk show to promote the new record and tour. While Iggy took care of the promotion, I spent some time New York nightclubbing and drinking beer with the delightful Joey Ramone. One night he took me to a party held in a loft apartment on Bleeker and Bowery Streets, a run-down dive of a place with an elevator that didn't work, and broken windows. Joey flashed one look at the assortment of users, lowbrows and deadbeats, and made straight back out the door with his girlfriend. I eyeballed Andy sitting in a corner of the room smoking what turned out to be a opium pipe, with his hand down some New York groupie's dress fondling her tit, and decided to stay and observe the action. Andy's bloodshot, hollow eyes registered recognition as I approached.

"Oh Alvin, you made it.. cool... have some of this."

Andy handed me the pipe and, without thinking, I took a deep hit. Within seconds of handing it back I broke into a cold sweat and very badly felt the need to vomit. Drowning in my own perspiration, I staggered across the room to the toilet. I don't know how long it took me to get there, but it felt like 50 years. When I pushed open the unlocked door, though, I saw the toilet was already occupied; there, humping some half-dressed peroxide starfucker up against a creaking sink, was the unmistakable visage of ex-New York Dolls guitarist Johnny Thunders.

Shit, I thought, I'm hallucinating, this just can't be.

Johnny looked back over his shoulder and without missing a beat asked, "What chew want, man?" *This* wasn't an illusion. Drug-induced hallucinations don't come with such authentic accents.

"I am so sorry to trouble you, but do you think I could possibly use that sink to vomit in?" I enquired in my best, polite Queen's English.

"Hey, take a look, I'm busy here... use the fuckin' bath, man," said Johnny.

And so I did. As Johnny Thunders continued to screw his loudly-appreciated chick, I threw up in the bath 'til there was nothing but bile, and my need to vomit subsided. I cleaned my face on a towel and looked back at Johnny for the last time.

"I'm sorry man," I said.

Johnny's final words on the matter displayed understanding. "Done it myself man... shut the door on yas ways out, willyas."

So I did, and rejoined Andy and his gum-chewing groupie.

"Guess what?" I said. "Johnny Thunders is fuckin' some chick in the toilet."

"Yeah, I know," replied Andy, pointing to the groupie sitting next to him. "It's her friend in there with him."

"Why the Hell didn't you warn me then, when you saw me going in there?"

"Oh come on man, where do you think you are... some Mayfair gentleman's club or something?"

He had a point.

Several hours had passed into our nine hour flight to Rio de Janeiro, and I was piecing together the last couple of weeks. Taking stock, drawing conclusions.

1 This was not really a band in the conventional sense. The power, the draw was Iggy Pop. Andy, Paul, Seamus and I were hired guns, necessary but expendable. If we fucked up – replaceable.

2 Everyone was covering their own asses. Self interest rules. Keep in with Jim, keep in with the management, keep your nose clean and secure your position. Don't make waves. Don't stick up for Andy if he gets found out… You may go down with him. All very alien to my previous band experiences, where being in group was like being in a gang. "You mess with my drummer, you mess with me, mate." But, this was not really a band in the conventional sense.

3 Certain crew members have an attitude. One or two of them have been with Iggy for a while. They had seen musicians come, musicians go. Since the Stooges, Iggy had put together numerous outfits for touring and recording. They knew that this year's band would most likely not be next year's band and had developed a frame of mind accordingly. It was understandable but, once again, contrary to my experience.

4 I didn't much like it.

Now I'm not complaining here, you understand. This is just observation. As a member of the Iggy Pop band I was well paid, well wined and well dined and put up in fine rooms in excellent hotels. But, there was a definite back-drop of insecurity to this set-up. A subtle shade of paranoia that, frankly, I felt was unnecessary. As Andy had pointed out back on that first beer-hiding, Hollywood afternoon when we had met with Iggy, "It's politics, man… fuckin' politics."

Our plane swooped down into Rio airport, its rubber wheels making contact with the sun-baked runway – the Iggy Pop bandwagon rolled into Brazil. We swapped our 747 for a DC9 and back up into the wide blue, our destination this time, São Paulo. Incredible scenery. Below me were the most amazing mountains, rivers, jungle and forest for as far as the eye could see. While I enjoyed my third cocktail up there, down below – somewhere – an Indian was hunting for dinner, chewing on his coca leaves with spear in hand as we, a degenerate bunch of half-cut rock musicians, glided over his head, oblivious.

A rapid descent into the largest city in the southern hemisphere – São Paulo has a population of over fifteen million – and we bade the attractive Brazilian airline stewardesses adieu. Andy reckoned he had joined the mile high club with the prettiest one of them… but, of course, no-one would believe him. This put McCoy into a funk as we boarded our waiting coach for the long and tiring journey to our hotel.

The promoter had booked us into a real classic. It looked liked a Warsaw tower block and, horror or horrors, had no room service, bar or swimming pool. Iggy told TM Henry this just wasn't good enough. Henry, in turn, ordered the promoter to find us something better – and quickly – as we were all tired and emotional, in no mood to be diplomatic with the locals.

Now, I know this may sound spoilt to some of you, but it's a serious issue! The promoter, when he booked the band, was given the hotel requirements and agreed to them. Then, he attempted to fob us off with accommodation that didn't reach those agreed standards, so he could pocket himself some extra money. He was pulling a number and, what's more, we knew it.

The promoter's response to Henry's reasonable request was to stomp up and down in the lobby, waving his arms around, speaking very quickly in Portuguese. I'm half-Portuguese myself, and though my understanding of the language is somewhat limited, I figured out he was basically telling us that we were a bunch of arrogant, spoilt, foreign bums and we should fuck off on the next possible flight home. I began to suspect this would end in tears.

Iggy was freaking out.

"What the fuck is he saying, Henry… tell him I'm tired, my wife and band are tired, and we want a better hotel… NOW!"

The promoter wouldn't listen, he was too far gone, graphically explaining in Portuguese where we should stuff our guitars, and what he thought of our crazy demands. Iggy decided to break this deadlock by breaking a low table in the lobby area with a swift stamp of his heavy right boot.

All Hell broke loose.

The hotel concierge leaped over the desk and waved his fist in Iggy's face, threatening all manner of physical retribution, in his native tongue. Iggy pushed him in the chest and looked set to lay him out, moving in for the kill. Henry got in between them, shouting in Glaswegian, which is far more difficult to understand than Portuguese, while the promoter went into Brazilian Expletive Overdrive. Suchi pleaded with Iggy to calm down, when suddenly, out of nowhere, just to add the finishing touches to the scene, a bunch of salivating local paparazzi entered the foyer and furiously snapped the ensuing chaos.

Welcome to Brazil.

Calm was restored eventually, with promises of payment for damages rendered, and an agreement to whisk us off to a new, improved hotel as fast as the coach could get us there.

The next day, the paparazzi's work appeared in a full-page spread. According to the Brazilian newspaper *Ilustrada*, "Rock star Iggy Pop physically assaults promoter over hotel accomodation and threatens to cancel show."

Amongst the text, sat five photos of Iggy in various states of exasperation, fist-waving, foaming at the mouth and threatening. That was hardly the kind of publicity we were seeking on our first day there.

Iggy Pop chega alegre, irrita-se com "flat", cancela show e estréia hoje

Da Reportagem Local

Fotos Luis Carlos Marauskas

O cantor norte-americano Iggy Pop, 41, um dos precursores do movimento punk, chegou ontem às 13h em São Paulo. O show de ontem à noite que o cantor faria no Projeto SP foi cancelado. Segundo Arnaldo Waligora, proprietário do Projeto SP, o cancelamento foi provocado pelo atraso na chegada do cantor. Iggy apresenta-se hoje e amanhã em São Paulo, terça e quarta no Rio de Janeiro e volta para um show extra no Projeto SP na quinta-feira.

Vestido com botas, calça e blusão de couro preto com desenhos brancos, cabelos longos e tingidos, Iggy estava bem diferente da imagem "clean" de dois anos atrás. Acompanhado pela mulher, Suchi, e mostrando bom humor, ele disse que a viagem tinha sido ótima e que estava "muito feliz" por estar no Brasil. Sobre o atraso de dois dias não soube dar explicações, sorriu e levantou os ombros. "Eu não sei."

Iggy disse que não terá muito tempo para conhecer o país e deverá viajar logo depois dos shows para o Canadá, para continuar a excursão mundial para promover o recém-lançado álbum "Instinct" (que está sendo lançado aqui pela Polygram). O bom humor começou a diminuir logo que chegaram ao hotel Victoria Place, no Itaim, zona sul. Segundo mas mesmo assim resolveu subir. Cerca de 20 minutos depois desceu, contrariado, para se encontrar com a banda que acabava de chegar. "Primeiro foi o problema do vôo, agora essa do hotel. Não suporto desonestidade. Não vamos ficar aqui. Não é ruim, mas não é hotel, é flat. Vocês sabem: como é. É frio, não tem serviço de quarto, cozinha, e tem uma construção do lado", disse para os músicos na calçada. Mais tarde a banda todos indo para o hotel Eldorado Higienópolis.

Segundo Arnaldo Waligora, "a origem toda do problema chama-se aeroporto Kennedy". "Até agora não entendi exatamente o que aconteceu", disse, referindo-se às dificuldades em encontrar passagens para todos os integrantes da excursão, que não aceitavam viajar separados. Quanto ao hotel, Waligora

O roqueiro norte-americano Iggy Pop expulsa o fotógrafo da Folha do carro que o levaria do aeroporto de Cpica para o flat; a seu lado está sua mulher, Suchi

disse que mora no Victoria e que ele é do mesmo nível, tanto em conforto quanto no preço, que a opção decidida no contrato. "Quis dar um tratamento diferenciado para eles e a transa dos caras é hotel. O Victoria é um flat", disse. Da banda que veio junto, apenas

Seamus Beaghen, particí da excursão que veio depois do "Blah, Blah, Blah", de 1986. Os mais são Andy Mc Coy (guitarrista Hanoy Rocks), Elvin Gibb (baix), ex-UK Subs) e Paul Garisto aterista, ex-Psychodelic Furs). Segdo Iggy, eles estão juntos há mas três semanas mas formar ......a ótima

banda. Nesse tempo, fizeram algumas apresentações na costa oeste dos EUA (Santa Bárbara, Los Angeles) e em Nova York, sempre em locais pequenos, para cerca de 200 ou 300 pessoas. Ele disse que o show vai ser "fucking good" e não quis adiantar o que vão tocar. "Você vai ter que ir lá para var ver."

Ingressos para ontem vão ser aceitos hoje

Quem comprou ingressos de pista para ontem poderá ver Iggy Pop hoje, amanhã ou quinta. Os ingressos de camarotes e cadeiras superiores são válidos apenas para o show de hoje. Quem tiver ingresso de pista para ontem e não puder ir ao show em outro dia, terá seu dinheiro de volta. O Projeto SP fica na r. Dr. Sérgio Meira, 238, tel. 826-5749, Barra Funda, zona central. Os ingressos custam Cz$ 3.000,00 (pista), Cz$ 4.000,00 (cadeira superior) e Cz$ 6.000,00 (camarote). Hoje e quinta-feira o show começa às 21h30. Amanhã, às 20h.

Mais calmo, Iggy deixa-se fotografar no hall do Flat Victoria Place fazendo pose, antes de subir ao quarto que tinha sido escolhido pelos promotores de seus shows

*

Our new hotel, the El Dorado Higienopolis, did indeed have room service, bar, and pool, and to the relief of all, harmony was restored.

That first South American night, we were all taken out for dinner to an excellent restaurant by our A&M Records (Brazil) company reps, Carlos and Renaldo. The wine flowed. Iggy impressed us all with his vast knowledge of South American geography and affairs, while I was awarded a Cuban cigar and fine cognac by Carlos, after informing him that my grandmother was, in fact, Brazilian. This was true, but I made a mental note to try the same thing

39

in all the countries we visited, "Sure, my grandmother is Greek, didn't you know?" in the hope of procuring the same response throughout the tour.

Next day, Andy and I went for a walk to try and get some feel for the city. São Paulo turned out to be a sprawling, industrial, heartless place. Walk around the hotel and it was large houses, fashionable shops and restaurants, chic, well-dressed women, and Armani-suited men driving expensive cars. Affluence ruled.

Walk on a little further, and it was a very different story. Streets of rubble, poor housing, dirty-faced, bare-foot kids, kicking around a football with dreams of escaping their circumstances, the Pele way. Poverty ruled.

This was a city where it was apparent that the gap between rich and poor was an ocean wide.

We had two nights to play at the 4,000 seater, São Paulo Projecto Theatre, entertaining the sons and daughters of the wealthy. The price of one of our tickets was more than a Brazilian manual worker could have hoped to earn in a month. With this in mind, Iggy shared his thoughts with the pampered, empty-eyed, dilettante crowd.

"Yeah, you've got money, alright... big cars, houses, servants... but really, you ain't got shit, you ain't got heart, you ain't got balls, you ain't got nuthin'."

He looks back at us.

"Play for these zombie motherfuckers, 'Your Pretty Rich Face Is Going To Hell'." .

The word 'rich' was added to the title for the rest of our Brazilian stay.

It struck me afterwards how strange it was that in the poorer countries of the world, the music that the richer nations consider low-brow and 'for the masses' – namely rock 'n' roll – has become the music for the wealthy and the elite. In the majority world, a ticket to a rock gig was as prestigious and expensive as a ticket to a black-tie classical performance or a night at the opera in, say, the USA or Western Europe. This was how things were, and despite our disapproval of this state of affairs, there was nothing we could do about it.

After catching the afternoon shuttle service for a short flight north on a Varig Airlines prop plane, we said goodbye to São Paulo and hello to Rio de Janeiro. Excitement built as we banked left over Sugarloaf Mountain, and the beauty of Rio was displayed for our inspection. Even normally gruff and sour-faced keyboardtek Mark Edwards had a smile on his face.

Our hotel was right on the Copacabana beach and Iggy, Andy and I didn't even bother to drop off our hand luggage in reception before, straight from the car, we took off across the white sand to the rolling turquoise ocean, whooping and yelling like excited school boys. We felt quite drunk on the glamour of Rio

A chilled bottle of champagne awaited me in my room, courtesy of A&M Records. After pouring a glass, I stepped out onto my balcony to survey the view. It was magnificent.

A trip around town had been set up for the evening by our Rio promoter, Arnoldo Walligora. We took a cable-car up Sugarloaf Mountain to watch an outdoor Samba show, comprising of gyrating, colourfully-dressed, dark-skinned dancers getting wilder and wilder as the various drums, whistles and instruments of the Brazilian band increased in tempo. The rhythm was hypnotic. As we sipped rum punches under the sheltering sky, one of the girl dancers grabbed our very English, beautifully-mannered soundman Tim Sunderland, and did her best to get him to join in. Tim made

Andy, Paul, Alvin and Iggy with a local woman in Rio

one or two stiff, awkward movements that bore no resemblance to dancing whatsoever, before becoming too embarrassed to continue any longer and returning to his seat to a burst of sympathetic applause from the understanding crowd. "Poor man... he must be English, sim?"

Drumtek Jos's succinct comment on the whole affair was, "Yes... very visual." Later, we drove along the gorgeous Copacabana shoreline. I pointed out the brown-eyed, bronze-skinned local goddesses to a nodding, smiling Iggy, and we stopped to sample some fresh coconut milk at a stall on the beach.

On the way back to the hotel, our driver pointed out a shanty city, high on a hill. A big, sprawling, ugly conurbation of corrugated iron, plywood shacks and dirt roads. No sanitation, no running water. None of the basics we take for granted in our homes, for those refugees of poverty up there. The driver informed us that two hundred and fifty thousand souls lived on that hill. He told us of a foreign film crew that went up there to make a documentary some months before, and had come back down stripped of everything but their underwear. Cameras, money and clothes all gone. He added that they were lucky to get back down at all... alive.

Somewhere between the roof-top bar and the ground floor of our hotel, on the way down for the sightseeing tour, Andy had disappeared from the elevator. He turned up later that night in my room, high as a kite on some locally available chemical, demanding that I give him my room service dinner so he could pass it out to the starving children of Rio, like some kind of Narcotic Jesus. I didn't mind him taking the food, but objected strongly when he snatched my duty free brandy from the table.

"That stays with me," I said, snatching it back.

Let them drink cognac... I don't think so!

Alvin and Andy on Copacabana beach in Rio

The next day, Jos told me that he saw Andy in the hotel lobby at about 4am, incoherently pleading with the receptionist to have a stuffed Armadillo, a set of kitchen knives and a vicious-looking machete procured from a street vendor paid for by the hotel and put on his room bill. The receptionist sensibly declined McCoy's request.

Gig day in Rio, and Andy was complaining that he was ill; Iggy had sussed the real problem, and was decidedly brittle with him. Henry read McCoy the riot act as we stepped out to play a pleasant show at our 3,000 seat modern auditorium venue, in front of a full house of Brazilian rock stars and glamour pussies.

Carlos and Renaldo – which, I got to say, sounds like a cabaret duo – turned up again to buy us yet another exquisite meal, and take us to what they assured us was the coolest night-spot in town, The Africa Club. This was full of catwalk models and other unbearables, flaunting their unwearables, along with a host of over-manicured local fashion victims. We made a hasty exit.

By the last day, my initial favourable impressions of Rio had changed. I'd come to realise that all that glitters is indeed not gold. Crime was endemic here, a consequence of the huge gulf between the haves and the have-nots, with daily murders, constant muggings and wanton acts of violence being committed in this visual paradise. Most of the women we had seen on the beach were stunning, but Carlos had warned us in São Paulo that nearly all of them were hookers, and that 90% of the prostitutes of Rio were now HIV positive.

Despite its outward beauty, in many ways Rio de Janeiro is an ugly and dangerous place.

We flew further south still, along the Brazilian coastline, turning west over Uruguay and touched down in the capital of Argentina, Buenos Aires. We were to play two shows there, with a night off to explore the city and enjoy our incredibly grand and elegant hotel, the Alva Palace. Stepped out for a stroll with Iggy and Suchi to find that sophisticated, attractive women abound among the graceful 18th century European-style architecture. A definite vibe of wealth and privilege to the place. The suburbs we drove through on our way in from the airport painted another picture.

Our friendly Argentinean promoter took us to a packed club that night, where a local band played Beatles and Stones covers, and the cocaine was flying. It was everywhere.

One of the local band member's girlfriends invited me backstage where a pile of coke the size of Mount Fuji sat atop a guitar case. "Help yourself," she said and I figured, 'when in Rome...' or indeed, South America... I re-enacted a certain scene from the movie, *Scarface*. Andy was in Nirvana, and Paul was digging the action too. Seamus stuck to vodka, the boring bastard, while Iggy and Suchi made a hasty retreat, as this kind of situation is an anathema to Iggy... far too tempting.

Fuelled by the endless supply of South American Marching Powder, and numerous beers, I joined the local band on guitar for an unusual – as in, semiconscious – fucked up version of 'I Wanna Be Your Dog'. I ended up playing 'til 7am, slaughtering a whole bunch of classic songs along the way. It was good, drug-induced fun.

The following afternoon, before the soundcheck, I cleared my head with a game of soccer with the promoter's staff and other locals. No 'hand of God' to help them this time, with us Brits thrashing them 5-1, while Iggy, who is crap at football, and Suchi, who thought we were playing cricket, yelled advice from the sidelines. Andy was replaced at half time for refusing to take off his cowboy hat when heading the ball, which Jos ruled was ungentlemanly conduct. For a New Yorker (and a drummer), Paul Garisto proved a handy goal-keeper, while defenders Jos and Henry sent up the long ball to Seamus, soundman Tim and I, so we could knock them in and shout, "Gotcha!"

National pride restored, we went on to play a blinder at the Obra Stadium.

Night of the Iguana... 4,000-plus crowd of hot-blooded, hot-headed Argentinean rock 'n' roll aficionados. Iggy was so delighted by their demonstrative, unrestrained response that he had us add an extra encore of 'I Feel Alright' and a fierce, rocking version of the Kingsmen's classic 'Louie Louie' – one of Iggy's favourite songs – as a thank you.

Hats off, then, to Buenos Aires. Hasta la vista, Argentina... over and out.

Canada. Iggy sat across from me in the lobby of the Four Seasons Hotel, Toronto, telling Paul about some one-legged girlfriend from his distant past.

"Yeah man, she was great. 'Jim,' she would say, 'let's fuck,' and she would lie back and take off her metal leg... which really turned me on."

Nearly two weeks had passed since that killer show in Buenos Aires. A short tour of Canada is all but over, and it's been a slog. Ottawa, Montreal, Cambridge and Windsor, Ontario. Plus a three day stint at Toronto's Club RPM, during which a camera crew came up from LA to film each night to splice together footage for a promo video for the next single release, 'High On You'.

The tour had its moments. Iggy losing his shoes after being dragged into the crowd on the last night, only to dive back into the audience, to emerge with a completely different pair, which didn't fit. A beer-drinking session at the Windsor Hilton with guitarist Izzy Stradlin from Guns N' Roses who had just finished a show across the Canadian border in Detroit, Michigan, opening up for born-again rockers Aerosmith. Saying hello to Neil Young in the Four Seasons bar and asking him to pass the peanuts... And that kind of thing.

After the spice of South America, Canada had proved a bland, lukewarm water kind of affair: we were glad to be splitting, England-bound.

As the limos pulled up in the Four Seasons forecourt to whisk us off to the airport, Iggy yelled across the lobby to Andy, "Hey Andy... ever screwed a chick with a limb missing?"

Andy pulled a look of pure disgust.

"Oh man, you're kidding. I couldn't go with a woman with no arms, or nothin'." This amused Iggy no end.

"Ha ha ha... you're a pussy, McCoy. You should try it... you'd like it."

Suchi and Alvin beneath Sugar Loaf mountain, Rio

DON'T LOOK DOWN

It was good to be back in London. Despite my years away in the USA, London still felt like home. On my first day there, I lunched at Le Gavroche restaurant, walked in St James's Park, and visited a friend for a nice cup of tea. It was very relaxed, very sedate, very English.

Wired was a weekly, Channel Four, British TV music show with a decent audience rating and a prime-time Friday night spot. A potentially good bit of promotion for our forthcoming UK winter tour. We had been booked to play five songs live in front of an invited crowd at Pinewood Studios in the heart of the Buckinghamshire countryside where the programme would be filmed for transmission at a later date. At rehearsals, Iggy got decidedly leery. The director wanted to use some flash bombs and firework effects to spice things up and that idea, along with the ridiculous, flashing disco-style lights, had made our singer a less than happy man. He decided to get things out into the open.

"Mr Director, where are ya?" Iggy called out through the microphone. A grey-haired, earnest gentleman with a clipboard stepped forward.

"How can I help you, Mr Pop?" the director gushed, putting on his best 'interested' veneer.

"You can help me by getting rid of all this shit," Iggy said, waving his hands in the direction of the effects. "And while you're at it, change these fuckin' Mickey Mouse lights, will ya."

The director was struck dumb by these flippant remarks concerning his carefully laid plans for a "splendid show." His assistant decided to speak on his behalf, "Er...actually, what we're trying to do here is make the whole thing more exciting." Iggy didn't say anything; he just fixed him with a look of perfect disdain. The director's assistant began to look decidedly uncomfortable.

"You... um... see, from a visual point of view, we are in need of something... well, how can I put it?..."

Intimidated by Iggy's gaze, his train of thought suffered a derailment until, eventually, he found what he considered to be an appropriate word.

"...Stimulating," he concluded, half smiling.

Oh shit! I looked at Paul, Paul looked at me, and we both looked at Iggy 'cos we knew now what was coming.

CRASH!

Iggy had launched his mike stand into the air and, with unerring accuracy, it had landed atop a camera, bounced off the cameraman's head, and smashed through a piece of plastic stage set. Both the director and his assistant looked ready to bolt.

It was then that Iggy let rip.

"You hire a rock 'n' roll singer and his band to perform and entertain, and then you insult them. You wanna see excitement...? You wanna see something stimulating...?" Iggy walked around the stage, kicking over amps, drum kit, set, and anything else in striking distance. "Is that fuckin' stimulating enough for ya?"

Iggy marched off to the dressing room with the band following behind. Ten minutes later, the director and his assistant entered our room, with metaphorical hats in hand. Iggy had won the day. There were no fireworks, no explosions, no disco lights, and we went on to play a blistering five song set, with Mr Pop giving a mind-blowing, high-kicking performance in front of, below and on top of the rolling, star-struck cameras.

The next day, we went to Reading.

Now, the Reading Festival is something of an English Summer institution. A three day musical extravaganza, played out in a huge field full of pharmaceutically-deranged, beer-guzzling punters all determined to have a bloody good time in knee-deep, rain-sodden Berkshire mud.

I hate festivals.

I hate the dirt, the squalor, the bad food and the never-ending wait to use a stinking, piss-flooded toilet. I avoid them like the plague. This time, though, as Iggy Pop's bassist, I was obliged to attend. This time, it would be a headline show, with The Ramones (hurrah!), The Wonder Stuff and Fields of the Nephilim, among others, warming up the crowd before us.

Now the Reading Festival wasn't always so rock-orientated. Started in the 60s as a summer showcase and August Bank Holiday weekend frolic, it originally catered for jazz and blues fans, with the occasional R & B act thrown in for good measure. Its creators, Jack Barry and the staff at the famed London Marquee Club, slowly decreased the amount of jazz and blues acts over the years, so that by the early 70s, Reading had become primarily a more commercial, money-spinning rock festival. The likes of Deep Purple and Free would guarantee far larger audiences than George Melly or Johnny Dankworth could ever hope to achieve. With the coming of punk rock, the Damned and the Stranglers amongst other new wave outfits – brought their own brand of high energy rock to the event. Despite a somewhat credible accusation that the Reading Festival was too conservative and too slow to bring new music and bands to its stage, it has generally managed to reflect popular tastes in contemporary music and achieve a balance of new and established groups in its annual line-up.

The Ramones were done. Our TM, Henry, stuck his head round our caravan dressing room door to inform us, "It's that time again... chop chop, laddies."

On the walk from the dressing room to the stage, we stopped a while for the press. A wall of photographers snapped away at us, while Iggy, with the band lined up behind him, posed and preened and played the rock star for the appreciative camera-carriers. Those flashes were so overwhelming that I was temporarily struck with a mild form of blindness. At stage side, my sight fully recovered, I thought, bloody Hell, there must be all of Southern England out there.

Well not quite, just 30,000 or so.

The show was good, real good. Here's what the British music weekly *Melody Maker* had to say:

> *"Dog, you f***ers — Dog!"* — a racing shambles of an encore, operas such as "No Fun" and "I Wanna Be Your Dog" and "Shake Appeal" are assaulting the night sky. If one finishes, Iggy bawls the hell out of the band (heroes each) till they start another. It's poetry on the pull. It ended sometime and we got a lift back with a woman whose eyes were closed and I should summarise the Friday at Reading *but Iggy tore the roof off the whole world.* The rest of it flew out through the gaping chasm he invented. It was guitars and it was ascension. Contemporary trends be scorned; this was Wagner. The final image is of Iggy still there, for a full minute defiantly dancing after the band have gone off, gesturing and pumping crudely, sacrificing himself at the altar of himself, *gone gone gone* on the breathtaking perverse dignity of rock 'n' roll. The last purist. The last terrorist. The only star. — **CR**

With the exception of the iffy Wagner reference, I couldn't have summed it up better myself.

The next day, it was Switzerland. Zurich, to be precise.

On the flight over, I noticed that Iggy was reading again. This time, it wasn't a book. I stepped over and sat in the empty seat beside him. "Hey Jim, what you got there?"

Iggy showed me the cover which read, *Zombie Cop.* It turned out to be a movie script.

"Yeah, Alvin," Iggy said, "they want me to play the lead part in this horror flick. I'm to be the zombie cop." He added dryly, "Big surprise, huh?"

"Well, what's it about?" I asked him.

"It's about a cop who takes so many drugs, he turns into a fuckin' zombie."

"I see. It's typecasting."

"Yeah, those fuckers in Hollywood have been reading my biography again."

Actually, Iggy did have a legitimate movie career of sorts. He had appeared in director Martin Scorsese's *The Color Of Money* as a pool-room hustler who came off second best to Tom Cruise, and as a hotel visitor in Alex Cox's *Sid and Nancy*. Iggy definitely had ambitions of big screen success but we both agreed that *Zombie Cop* wasn't really the vehicle.

Another open air festival, but the civilised Swiss have the right idea with this one. Instead of a mud-caked piece of farm land stuck in the middle of nowhere – Woodstock has a lot to answer for – the Winterthur Festival was set in a beautiful wide cobblestoned city street complete with a baroque marble fountain at one end with the stage, PA and lights at the other. The surrounding buildings were straight out of a Bavarian fairy tale and the well-behaved, well dressed crowd of 8,000 provided appreciative, enthusiastic applause throughout our headline performance. No beer can missiles nor plastic bottles of warm piss heading stagewards that night. A more serene, gliding show than the previous evening's Reading appearance, played out in the warm summer Swiss night.

Afterwards, Sabina, our promoter, handed me several bars of delicious Swiss chocolate and a bottle of cognac. That morning, when she met us at the airport, I had casually mentioned that the combination of brandy and chocolate was one of my favourites. Sabina's gift was indicative of the thoughtful nature of all those involved in the Winterthur Festival; it was such a contrast to the 'treat the bands like shit', 'pack 'em in', 'rip 'em off' attitude exhibited at most festivals. It was a little gem.

Okay, Friday was Reading, Saturday Zurich, so Sunday just had to be... Tel Aviv.

A painless four hour hop on an El Al 767 from the land of hard cheese and chocolate to the land of prophets and Intifada. Through Israeli customs without a hitch and on to the hotel which, as in Rio, overlooked the beach. The view from my window was just as scenic too, with the foaming green-blue Mediterranean lapping up onto the hot sand directly below. To my right stood a mosque which seemed to be in the process of restoration by workmen wearing the distinctive red or black-checked Palestinian head-dress. To my left was the exotic, busy Arab quarter, and jutting out into the sea, the 4,000 year old port of Jaffa.

In the morning I joined Iggy, Suchi and the rest of the band and crew for an especially chartered coach ride to Jerusalem. Iggy was excited. He'd never visited this land before and he peppered our tour guide with all kinds of questions as the vehicle made its way along the dry and dusty road to Jerusalem.

Upon entering the city we stepped from the air-conditioned coach into the burning sun and saw the 16th century city walls of the Ottoman Sultan

Andy and Alvin at the Wailing Wall, Jerusalem

Suleiman the Magnificent, still sturdy and strong despite the passing of centuries. On to the Wailing Wall, guarded by soldiers in the olive green uniforms of the Israeli People's Army, with some so young and fresh faced that they looked better suited to carrying school books than weapons of war. Pretty, young, bright red-lipsticked girls too, with battle fatigues, Uzis and Chanel earring combinations... more manicured than martial. We passed the remnants of Solomon's Temple and looked down on the Messiah's Gateway from the Mount of Olives. As our tour guide led us through the labyrinth of dark back streets in the Arab section, I noticed he wore a shoulder holster containing a lethal-looking hand gun beneath his jacket. The Intifada – the Palestinian uprising against those they consider occupiers and oppressors – was still in full effect and these streets were potentially dangerous.

Lunch was at a small, basement Arab restaurant. The owner, having been informed of our arrival ahead of time, anxiously hurried us into the building pulling down a metal shutter behind him. We feasted on grilled fish, kebabs and falafel washed down with hot, sweet tea, and for dessert, a waiter passed over a Hooka (Arabian water pipe) for us to smoke from. Andy's eyes lit up but quickly extinguished again when he was told the one inch block of matter being lit in the pipe was tobacco, and not something stronger. Even so, if you took a big hit from it, drawing the grey smoke deep into your lungs, you certainly got an interesting sensation of elevation followed by several seconds of disorientation.

Iggy asked our guide about the nervous disposition of our restaurant owner-host. "He's worried because of the Intifada," he answered. "He's a Palestinian and, as such, is supposed to boycott trade to outsiders until the Intifada is lifted."

"What would happen if word got out he'd broken the Intifada by giving us this lunch?" Iggy inquired.

The guide put his right hand under his left ear, drew it across his throat, and imitated the sound of a razor cutting flesh.

"We would find his body in the gutter," he replied.

We left the restaurant owner and his staff a very, very good tip, "Don't risk your lives making lunch for a bunch of fuck-ups like us again. Okay?"

We had not come to Israel just for the sightseeing – there was work to be done. Two shows on consecutive nights at the Cinerama Theatre a mile or so from the beach in Kaufman Street.

The first night they were still chanting, "We want more," a full half hour after we had left the stage, having already played four encores.

On the second night, we added 'China Girl' and 'Sixteen' to the set – learned during a longer than usual soundcheck – with Iggy touching the faces of the sexually glowing shapely jail-bait at the front of the stage. Delivering the lines, "I must be hungry, 'cos I go crazy over your leather boots... Sweet sixteen..." with a perfect degree of desperation and desire.

A bunch of those stage-front beauties were waiting for us in the lobby on our return to the hotel. Suchi was still in transit, so Iggy took advantage, laying a long deep kiss into the lipstick mouth of one of these fab teenies and copping a feel of tit. It was furtive and fumbling, and Iggy knew it was going no further.

Paul grabbed a dark-skinned Sudanese-looking girl and whisked her off to his room, while another ran up to me and threw her arms around my neck. She was blue-eyed with child-bearing hips. Real pretty; but must have been all of 15 years young.

Just as my hormones were about to stage a coup d'état on my morals, Henry walked by and whispered the words, "Statutory rape," into my left ear. He was right. It wasn't worth it. A couple of members of the rockabilly band The Stray Cats were put on just such a charge after being caught with underage girls in Tokyo a few years previously. They had a tough time in police custody, suffered the indignity of the rock 'n' roll child molester world headlines, and were banned from playing in Japan.

Who needs that kind of grief? The sad truth is, some do. Or, rather, they are willing to take the risks that come with heeding the sirens' song.

Okay, let's cut to the chase here; you've had some drugs and rock 'n' roll, let's deal with the sex.

אבו־איאד: הכרזת העצמאות תכיר בישראל

ערא פאת דורש ב"לה מונד": "פדרציה ירדנית־פלסטינית
עם או בלי חוסיין, לצד ישראל". חוסיין הציע: איחוד
מדינות ערב עם פלסטין, דוגמת הקהיליה האירופית

חכם ראש בהקרינת הבכורה של סרט הפולחן האמריקני "המענקים", חזה כולם לעיני סרט, מי עשה את שיר הנושא למינט, ולגמרי...

The accepted wisdom seems to be that we rock musicians have become the new barbarians, raping and pillaging our way across the nations, wading waist-deep, nightly, in a sea of young nubile flesh. There is a degree of truth to this; all myths have a basis in fact. Certainly, the sexual adventures of bands like the Rolling Stones are well-documented and have advanced and hardened this opinion. The Stones 1972 American Tour movie, *Cocksucker Blues* provides all the proof needed to make the New Barbarian tag stick, with its famous graphic, sleazy sex scenes.

Stomping across the world at the same time, coming on like pre-Raphaelite bootboys, Led Zeppelin had also acquired a well-earned, well-remembered reputation for carnal exploits of the bizarre kind. An anecdote

51

concerning a Zep roadie with more imagination than sense, a compliant groupie and a freshly caught baby shark, still does the rounds in the rock biz and has become a legend of sorts.

Did it happen…? Well, maybe. Sometimes that kind of bizarre and lewd behaviour still happens. But it happens much less these days than people are prepared to believe. With the coming of HIV and Aids awareness in the 80s, the sexual excesses of the 60s and 70s have largely withered. Today's musicians are laying their lives on the line when they attempt to imitate the ways of the previous generation of touring rock 'n' rollers. The highest penalty paid for sleeping around, is no longer a dose of clap and a fortnight off the Jack Daniels whilst the antibiotics take effect. Tour sex has become carnal Russian roulette. With 'safer sex' now the norm, the 'quickie' in the back of the tour bus, or in the dressing room showers, is increasingly behaviour of the past.

Of course, Iggy is a veteran of those Hell-raising days of yore. His past excessive enjoyment of flesh, drugs and the rock 'n' roll lifestyle had also contributed to the mythology. Henry had told me about the bad old days before Suchi entered Iggy's life. Of having to deal with Iggy's seemingly endless stream of female companions and one night stands. Of the crazed 4am phone calls commanding Henry to come and eject so-and-so from his employer's hotel room after the volatile cocktail of opiates, liquor and sexual familiarity had finally taken their toll.

As with the drink and drugs, when it came to sex and touring, Iggy had turned it all around. Despite the occasional lingering kiss with strangers, his wife Suchi was, to my knowledge, his only lover on the road. They travelled everywhere together, constant companions, and Iggy seemed perfectly at ease with this situation.

Paul and Seamus being both young and single, with a healthy interest in female companionship, found occasions when the situation and the inclination were conducive, and acted accordingly. Andy, as in most things, worked on the principle that excess was not enough. He did show a degree of discrimination in these matters of the flesh, though, and on some occasions even acted with a little decorum.

And me…? I can be as tempted by the fruit of another as the next man. Seven months on the road without a wife or the semblance of an orderly home life can test even the most faithful of married men. But, married I am and, as such, I'll stick with the late Lenny Bruce's contention that all confessions of infidelity are a sophisticated form of sadism.

The bottom line is that if you want to fuck around, you can find just as many possible situations in the office, the factory, the local pub or bar, as you can on a rock 'n' roll tour… You only have to look.

The Mediterranean part of the tour was taking on a definite classical flavour. It was just a two hour flight from Israel, with its rich history and religious significance, to Athens, the cradle of democracy and the home of Western philosophy.

Don't go looking for no latterday Platos or Aristotles there nowadays, though. The modern Athenians are far too busy driving cabs, running bars and restaurants, and selling bad souvenirs, to be bothered with such questions as the ideal relationship between citizen and state. Or the true division between spirit and matter.

Athens today is a crowded, polluted metropolis full of drachma-loving merchants. However, from the vantage point of our roof-top hotel swimming pool I could see a relic, a reminder of Athens's glory days, set high up on the Acropolis, glowing gold in the afternoon sun like some Hellenic beacon. Iggy joined me to marvel at this white marble wonder of the classical age. The Parthenon.

"That's really beautiful, man... really beautiful."

It was an extraordinary sight; we feasted on it until the spell was broken by Henry's arrival and his announcement that it was time to sing for our supper.

That night, we played under the stars. An open air show at the Apollo football stadium on the outskirts of the city.

On our arrival, I took a walk through the labyrinth of changing rooms, offices and corridors that made up our backstage area. Up and out onto the pitch to check out the pre-gig situation. A stage had been set up at the half-way line with 12,000 Athenians crammed into the space in front of the stage and up into the main stand.

There were a lot of illegal entries that night. I saw at least 400 desperados clamber over the 15 foot barbed wired wall at the back of the stand before leaping down into the arms of their cheering friends below. It was a miracle that none of the ouzoed-out Greeks broke their necks during those gymnastics.

Oh, well... fuck it. We would get paid whether they'd bought tickets or not. The more the merrier.

It was a perfect show in just about every way. A real trouser-bustin', Homeric epic of a gig. We had drama when Iggy threw himself head-first from the stage into a sea of hands, eventually sinking without trace. The audience refused to hand him back and hard man Jos was forced to wade in to pull him out.

We had tragedy. Or, at least, near tragedy when Andy messed up the solo in 'China Girl' and Iggy almost decapitated him with the mike stand.

Comedy. When my trouser button flew off and, unable to prevent my strides from falling down around my ankles as it requires both hands to play the guitar, I suddenly found myself playing in my underwear.

And, last but not least, there was triumph, when 'I Gotta Right' blasted from the speakers at ramming speed and the sons and daughters of Athens, as one, surrendered their hearts to us with a roar loud enough to be heard on Mount Olympus.

Euripides and his Trojan women, be damned...! This *was* theatre.

Our delighted promoter, a large jolly woman with the impossible name of Dozie Panayiotopoulou, took us to an outdoor restaurant later that night for dinner. Iggy held court at one end of the table with Suchi beside him, her dark eyes sparkling in the candlelight. The food and wine put smiles on our faces as we sat and discussed the gig, learned Greek swear words from Dozie, and laughed at Andy's stories of past drug-induced mayhem.

Like the show, it was perfect. The air was warm, the bright moon was high, and an intense feeling of satisfaction descended upon me. I'd often contemplated why I'd become a musician. Often wondered why I loved music, touring and the musician's life so much, with all its difficulties and uncertainties. That night, under the Athenian stars, it became very clear why… It was so that I could be a part of such moments as these.

Come the morning, we said our goodbyes to Dozie and our new Greek friends and boarded the plane that would take us back to those United States of America. As the big bird rattled and shook along the runway, picking up speed for our ascent, I felt sadness at having to leave this part of the world. I was not much looking forward to returning to America, to the harsh slog of an American tour and, as the plane finally lifted off the runway and climbed for the clouds, I didn't look down.

Alvin with Joey Ramone at the Reading Festival

BOWIE, TEXAS AND THE ALAMO

We were back in the Big Apple. Back in the welcoming arms of the Mayflower Hotel, with an invitation to go visit Mr and Mrs Osterberg at their apartment and have some dinner.

Henry, Andy, Seamus and I caught a cab on Central Park West and headed off for the Iggy Pop homestead situated in that area of the city which New Yorkers refer to as Alphabet City – the lower East Side. Alphabet City doesn't have the affluence or pretensions of the West side of town but it does have the artists, the writers, the Bohemians and, therefore, the reputation as a neighbourhood of the fashionable.

Iggy's apartment was a penthouse affair, atop a classic art deco skyscraper and, on entering, he gave us a warm welcome and took us on a tour of his home. He showed us his work room with an eight-track recording facility, guitars and a microphone all permanently set up so Iggy could go in to put down new ideas for songs at any hour, as the inspiration took him.

Another room had been set aside for the hanging and display of his paintings. Iggy is a keen painter and he went through the ideas and circumstances behind each picture as we inspected them and offered our opinions. There were Jackson Pollack style splashes of oil on canvas and Picasso-esque portraits of Suchi and friends. I particularly liked, and remember, a vivid abstract representation of a wild dog leaping in mid-air. It had an appealing naive charm, as did all of Iggy's paintings.

The main room had ethnic print furniture with African and South American native artefacts dotted around. The walls were glass, giving an incredible all round view of the Manhattan skyline. Iggy took us out onto the balcony to point out the Empire State and Chrysler buildings sparkling in the distance.

"What a great place," I said.

Andy dug it too. "Jim... This is fuckin' beautiful."

"Yeah. We like it. You know, for a long, long time, I didn't have a home of my own. I lived in hotels and rented places. Until Suchi came along, I felt no need to put down roots and deal with stuff like buying furniture... You

know, putting out the trash, doing the shopping, that kind of thing. Now, though, I'm real proud of this place. It's good to have a home."

Iggy's home was a cool place; it was unpretentious with a good feel to it. I was glad to have had the opportunity to visit.

When Paul turned up, we all made our way around the block to Iggy and Suchi's local Italian for huge plates of pasta, washed down with light, crisp white wine. Iggy chided me when I started to flag with my king-size portion of seafood spaghetti.

"Hey, Alvin... Eat up that pasta. Y'gonna need all the energy you can get for this coming part of the tour!"

It was sound advice, alright. Iggy knew the coming weeks would prove tough on us all. He had been through it so many times before. After the excitement of recent gigs in scenic locations such as Athens and Rio De Janeiro, we were now looking at a two month trek across North America, playing shows in places such as Columbus, Ohio, Charlotte, North Carolina and Winnipeg, Manitoba. Energy-sapping, meat-and-potato shows with very little glamour and gruelling big bus drives in between.

A long tour of the USA can really chew up a band and spit it out. It's so fucking big. I'd done two month-long tours of the States with the UK Subs where we had flown from city to city and both had nearly killed me. Chances are this was the time when the discipline would go, when you'd start to lose your grip and grow sick of the playing, the travelling and all those around you.

It all started the following day, right there in New York City at The Pier, an 8,000 punter outdoor venue that resides by the water's edge of the East River on East 67th Street. It's a big, big all-seater with an aircraft carrier parked alongside it and a stage large enough to accommodate the New York Philharmonic and still have room for more.

Good. The bigger the stage, the less chance that Iggy will knock out my teeth or take a chunk out of my skull with his twirling, flying mike stand routines. He had come close to it a couple of times, at previous shows, and I felt it was only a matter of time before, in one of his rock-inspired spasms, he did me some serious damage.

The dressing room was a caravan in the backstage area containing the requisite food, drink and towels. Our support band for the evening was Jane's Addiction, an LA based up and coming attraction. I made sure I got to the venue earlier than usual to catch their performance, and Henry told me that they would be our opening band for the first third of the tour. For their encore, they took out a plastic bin and hammered on it with drumsticks whilst lead singer Perry spun around the stage making up lyrics and delivering them with a voice of pure venom. They were brilliant and, as they came offstage, I told them so. I was walking down the steps with them to the backstage area just as Iggy, Andy, Paul and Seamus arrived.

In the caravan, Iggy had some news.

"Bowie's here."

Cool. David Bowie was there to check out the band... That *was* news. But Iggy's voice betrayed unease at his old friend's presence.

"He'll hate it, or at least he'll hate me."

What? I couldn't believe this.

"What d'you mean, he'll hate you?"

"He won't like what I'm wearing and the direction I'm taking... He'll hate it. You know the guy comes on like a fuckin' rich Swiss banker nowadays... He lives in Montreux for fuck's sake."

As we ran on, like night-walking cheetahs, to face the crowd, I spotted Bowie standing with Suchi, stage right. I had dug Bowie a lot in the early 70s when he came on like a dream as Ziggy Stardust and enhanced my teenage anxieties with anthems like 'Rebel Rebel' and 'Rock 'n' Roll Suicide'. But after *Young Americans,* I had lost interest in his music, and the recent stuff I had heard from the Glass Spider Tour was pretty awful. Still, I was more than a little nervous to be eye-balled so closely by this star.

The show seemed to be going splendidly with the last song in sight and a favourable reaction from what is a notoriously tough, New York crowd.

Then Andy goes and commits the unforgivable sin of losing the plot guitar-wise in 'Winners and Losers'. He made the mistake of playing a secondary part four bars too early. Iggy turned on Andy with laser eyes of loathing.

"You stupid asshole motherfucker!"

Bewildered by this assault, Andy shrugged his shoulders and played on. Iggy wasn't satisfied by this response and hurled his mike stand at Andy, catching him painfully across the fingers of his note-playing hand. Rightly furious, Andy pulled off his guitar, smashed it to the floor and walked offstage, leaving the rest of the band to finish up whilst Iggy screamed blue murder at Andy through the microphone.

"Come back here, you pussy! You motherfuckin' asshole... You little rock 'n' roll fucker!"

Backstage, things got worse. The crowd were demanding an encore, but Andy had locked himself in the dressing room and was refusing to come out. Henry pleaded with Andy through the caravan door.

"Andy... Andy, come on. This here crowd wants an encore and we're all waiting for you."

Andy yelled back, "Fuck the crowd! I ain't playing with that cunt... He could have broken my hand out there."

"Andy, please... Andy, listen... You know Jim gets crazy on stage. He don't mean anything by it... He doesn't know what he's doing half the time!"

Andy was not convinced. "Fuck off! I'm not coming out."

It was not looking good.

The crowd were going nuts and our promoter, Ron Delsener, was worried that they would take the place apart if we didn't go back on soon. Iggy had calmed down somewhat since coming offstage, and Henry convinced him that some pride had to be swallowed. Iggy walked over to the caravan door.

"Hey, Andy... it's Jim... I'm sorry. You were right and I was wrong, okay? Now get your ass out here and let's blow this place apart!"

Andy slowly unbolted the door and, nervously, stepped out. Iggy hugged him and together we raced back on stage. As Iggy had predicted, we blew The Pier apart with a superfine version of 'Shake Appeal'.

Back in the dressing room, as we towel-dried off the sweat of the gig and drank beer, the door opened and in walked David Bowie. He was in good shape. Tanned, healthy and wealthy-looking, dressed in an amphetamine-blue designer suit and black turtle-necked top. Must be all that clean Swiss air, skiing and money.

"Hello there, Jim. Good gig. Good gig. Really liked this new band of yours."

Iggy, rather dryly, answered, "Thanks... I'm so glad you liked it."

"No, really. It's a great band you have here. Lots of energy and good players."

The atmosphere was somewhat strained. I handed Bowie a beer in the hope of improving things, and Iggy introduced us to him one by one. He'd even heard of the UK Subs. "Yeah. I remember your lot... Ha ha ha... Tough mob. All leather, studs and dyed hair... Ha ha ha. Good band, though. Lots of energy."

"Yeah," I said, "lots of energy."

I couldn't get over the blokeishness of the man. I guess he was really trying his best to be one of the boys, to abandon his superstar persona, but we, that is Iggy and the band, were snubbing him. It was as though the five of us, without a word having been said, had collectively decided to reject his overtures of bonhomie and act in the coolest possible manner towards him. Like the others, I just couldn't help myself.

Now, by Iggy's own admission, Bowie is supposed to be his best friend. They had first met at the famed New York night club Max's Kansas City in 1971. Max's was the New York musicians' hang-out and that night 17 years ago, there was the cream of the '70s musical aristocracy holding court. Before Lou Reed could finish telling Bowie a story about some junkie he knew who injected smack through his forehead, Iggy had jumped in and introduced himself. He and Bowie had hit it off. Bowie couldn't help liking the intelligent, ragged, funny little guy with the broken teeth and Iggy was flattered at Bowie's praise of his work and the English rock star's knowledge of the Stooges' Elektra albums.

In turn, Bowie had introduced Iggy to his manager Tony de Fries who signed Iggy up for his Mainman Management Company and promptly got Iggy and The Stooges a two album worldwide deal with CBS. It was Bowie who mixed the only record to make it out of that deal, *Raw Power*. And it was Bowie who was steadfast and loyal to Iggy when the quaaludes, downers and booze led to his prolonged stay in the Neuro-psychiatric Institute at the University of California, Los Angeles.

When Iggy was pronounced fit and well again, the two friends lived together in Berlin. During this time, Bowie worked on and produced one of Iggy's finest album achievements, *The Idiot*. Bowie went on to produce and contribute to two further Iggy records, *Lust for Life* and *Blah Blah Blah*, a continuation of a fruitful, 15 year long artistic and personal relationship.

In various press interviews, Iggy has said that Bowie was the first person in the business to treat him with dignity, and treat his ideas with respect. That Bowie had rescued his career and pleaded his cause when all others had looked down upon him as a dangerous lunatic.

Yet, in that dressing room at The Pier in New York City, all I saw was indifference on Iggy's part. Where was the warmth and the open display of friendship and affection I had expected? Had they fallen out recently? Could it be that Bowie had slated Iggy's new record in the press? I couldn't stand this uncomfortable situation any longer and went and joined the liggers outside the caravan to shake some hands and shoot the breeze.

One by one, the rest of the band joined me, leaving Iggy and Bowie together in the dressing room. When I re-entered the caravan half an hour or so later, the whole atmosphere had transformed. Iggy was drinking wine and smiling, attentively listening to Bowie talking about his new project, the formation of the band Tin Machine.

"Yeah, Jim, guess what? I've got your old rhythm section of Hunt and Tony Sales in on this one."

Iggy liked that idea. "Cool. Yeah. Very cool."

As an old Brooklynite friend of mine would have said, "Go figure!"

One minute it's detachment and disregard. The next, it's enthusiastic talk about forthcoming projects. I concluded that the relationship between Iggy Pop and David Bowie is somewhat more mysterious and complex than I could have anticipated.

The next day, the band were delighted to see Jim Boatman back at the steering wheel of the big bus.

"Hey, Mr Boatman! How's it going?"

"Not too bad… Hey, I see y'all gonna be playin' down in mah neck o' the woods on this here tour!"

"That's right, Jim… Nashville, Tennessee. Can't wait!"

"I better get me on my CB right now and warn the good God-fearin' citizens of Nashville to lock up their daughters."

"Oh, come on, Jim. You wouldn't wanna spoil our fun."

"I'm just jokin' with y'all now. I sincerely hope you get all the pussy down there you can handle… Just none of y'all go fuckin' my girlfriend… y'hear."

As well as having genial Jim Boatman back on board, our crew had expanded to 12 with the additions of a lighting man, Richard Gallup, lighting rigger Chip, monitor engineer Nick Bruce-Smith, merchandising salesman Marty Lawrence and new guitartek, Slouch. Mark Edwards had been promoted from guitartek to Production Manager and keyboard roadie… Sorry, I mean keyboardtek.

This lot would be travelling on a separate crew bus, with the equipment following on behind in a truck a city-block long driven by a man no-one in the band ever got to meet.

Newark, Porchester and Boston followed. Three okay-let's-go-do-it East Coast dates. Then, on Saturday 17 September we waved Mr Boatman goodbye for a while at Boston Airport, and boarded a Delta Airlines jet going south-west to Dallas-Fort Worth, Texas.

This was going to be a big one. A five band line-up at Texas Stadium, the home of the Dallas Cowboys football team. The Smithereens would be opening proceedings with Ziggy Marley on second, the Iggy Pop band in the middle slot and Guns N' Roses and INXS to follow.

As we limo-luxuriated along the airport freeway toward the stadium, Iggy made a few last minute changes to the set, swapping songs around and subtracting some of the slower numbers. We had been allocated an hour on stage here, as opposed to our usual 90 minute show, and we wanted to make a powerful and direct impact. Our friendly limo driver quickly looked back over his shoulder at us and said, "Texas Stadium is straight up ahead, fellas. Ain't she a beaut?"

I lowered my window and shoved my head out to have a look. There it was, big as life with 60,000 Texans, no doubt all in stetsons, waiting for us to go entertain them. This really was top shit.

A short while later, we reached the security barriers where uniformed armed guards signalled to the driver to come to a halt. One approached the limo.

"Okay, gen'lemen. Let's see your passes. Iggy Pop band, huh? Okay, please follow the signs with home team written on 'em. Have a good show, now!"

A real surge of excitement as we drove on deep into the subterranean heart of this amazing structure. We stepped out of the limos to find two waiting officials who led us through the seemingly endless maze of corridors to an elevator that took us to our dressing room high up in the stadium. What a view! Our dressing room turned out to be one of those windowed commentary boxes where the likes of NBC's John Madden shares his thoughts on the grid-iron action with football fans across the nation.

Way down below, Ziggy Marley had taken the stage to the ear-splitting sound of 60,000 voices raised in unison, all welcoming the son of the great reggae songsmith.

Slash and Izzy from Guns N' Roses stopped by to share a beer. This was to be their final performance of a non-stop, year-long tour to promote their massive selling album *Appetite for Destruction*. It showed. But despite the tired, glazed eyes and snow-white skin, they carried themselves like the 'rock stars on the up' that they had become. Both were a picture of seedy, sartorial elegance in their scuffed-up cowboy boots, tight ripped-up jeans and mixture of leather, silks and tat. They brought a touch of swagger and exaggerated glamour to our dressing room.

Izzy Stradlin was the first to speak. "Like, what are you guys up to later?"

"We're staying at the same hotel as you, I think," Andy told him. "Hey, Henry, where are we staying?"

Henry was pissed off. "The Four Seasons... That's the fifth time I've told you that today. Don't ask again."

"Yeah, right, The Four Seasons."

"Right, good," said Izzy, obviously pleased. "Come up to Slash's room. We're gonna have a party."

"Cool, man... Hey, you got any smack?" asked Andy, true to form.

Slash turns to me. "What's the first thing you do when you get up in the morning?"

"Get dressed, have a piss, wash... The usual stuff."

"Huh... Really?"

"Yeah."

"The first thing I do when I get up is reach for the vodka."

"What? First thing when you wake up?"

"Yeah... You don't think I've got a drink problem, do ya?"

Thankfully, before I could answer that one, Iggy came over to declare it was time to shake some action.

We went down in the elevator and ran into INXS's Michael Hutchence, looking every inch the pop star in a fetching open-necked Paul Smith shirt underneath a pea-green velvet suit. Hair by someone expensive by the looks of it, and the obligatory ultra, ultra-gorgeous model-type on his left arm. I gave him a handshake and a quick hello before climbing the ramp up onto the side of the stage, where he wished me luck.

"Oh, me and Michael go back... minutes," I admitted to an impressed, then just as quickly unimpressed Henry.

It was time for the work in hand. What a sight! A wall of humanity without faces stretching from the front of the stage up into the gods and surrounding us on all sides. A deafening sound as we stepped onto the boards with guitars at the ready and Iggy gesturing to the audience to stand and prepare to receive.

The crowd's roar was extraordinary in its intensity and volume; I knew then what it must be like to be a Cowboys' receiver scoring a touchdown, and why you would want to repeat the experience time and time again.

The new, meaner, leaner set worked well. 'Passenger' unfurled slowly like a carpet being unrolled for inspection with Seamus's keyboard parts punching holes in the rhythm. In the middle – the 'la la, la la... la la la la... la' part of the song – the band instinctively stop playing leaving Iggy and the arm-waving 60,000 to sing on their own for a while until Paul's dramatic drum fill brought us crashing back into the riff once more.

During 'No Fun', Andy spotted that two walkways were running along the left and right sides of the stage, blocked off by wooden barriers. These walkways were supposed to be reserved for the headliners INXS, but Andy wasn't having any of that shit. With a swift kick, he knocked down the obstruction closest to him. Iggy joined Andy and together they took off along this narrow pathway dancing and barging into each other like a couple of crazies.

I was watching all of this on a huge screen to my right for the poor sods in the cheap seats who didn't stand a snowball's chance in Hell of catching the action on the actual stage. Iggy and Andy looked great.

At The Four Seasons Hotel that night, Andy and I attended the Guns N' Roses party in Slash's room. Not only had G N' R been booked in there, but

INXS also had rooms at this hotel. As a result, there were beautiful women all over the place. In the lobby, in the elevators, in the corridors and, especially, in Slash's room. On entering the party, a topless blond bombshell with a soft Texan accent sashayed up to Andy and me, and asked if we would both be "so kind as" to feel her tits.

"Er... Now why exactly would you want us both to feel your tits?"

Her answer was perfectly logical, "Because I've just had them surgically enlarged and I wanted y'all to tell me if they feel real or not?"

Not only did eager and willing doll-faced sex kittens abound, but there were also drugs aplenty for the asking. Coke, hash and grass for the lightweights; smack and crack for the hardened professionals. Andy fell into the latter category. With my lingering memories of the opium pipe/Johnny Thunders/vomit fiasco back in New York, I decided on some of Slash's vodka and an occasional toke of a grass-filled joint.

As the night progressed, more hedonistic adventurers arrived. With the passing of the midnight hour, the action grew increasingly unhinged. There was projectile vomiting out of windows, blow-jobs à la carte, roadies fucking in wardrobes and, in general, scenes so weird and twisted that the Marquis de Sade would have fled in embarrassment.

Now it could be that these Rabelaisian recollections have been exaggerated somewhat by the late hour, the grass and the vodka, but if that is the case, it's not by much. Even Axl Rose, G N' R's rebel without a cause, reached the point where he could no longer handle the decadence and fled to the sanctuary of his room. This really was a throwback to the 'more sex, more drugs and fuck tomorrow' rock 'n' roll tour parties of the 60s and 70s.

That night, whilst the clean-living INXS got their beauty sleep, G N' R were more than happy to be the standard bearers for the New Barbarians. Certainly, under their auspices, many got laid and stoned, and a select few turned blue.

But as I had watched the events around me, I couldn't help thinking it was all just a desperate attempt to keep alive, against the odds, the mortally wounded, discredited rock 'n' roll myth. It was appropriate that this had occurred in the state of Texas. With all its false glamour and too-fast-to-live, too-young-to-die fatalism, that night reminded me more of a last stand than a revival.

With Slash's hotel room, the Alamo.

ACROSS THE USA

It was early morning in Orlando, Florida and the bedside phone was begging to be picked up and answered.

I knew it was Henry calling because the ringing had a self-important tone which grew in volume the longer you left it. I'd had a late night, was suffering a hangover from Hades and really did not give a shit.

Ring ring... Ring ring... Persistent bastard. Okay, better pick up the phone and deal with this now, I reasoned with myself. "Hello."

"Alvin. It's Henry."

"Yeah?"

"You were supposed to be in the lobby ten minutes ago."

"So fuckin' what?"

SLAM.

Ladies and gentlemen, welcome to the ass-end of a long and tortuous tour of the United States of America. Yes, once again, the lack of sleep, the number of shows required, combined with the huge distances covered, had led to a normally reasonable musician becoming an abusive bastard. And it wasn't just me who was suffering from that particular malady. When I finally made it down to the hotel lobby with my suitcase, just about everyone in the band was in some kind of funk. Seamus and Paul were moaning to Henry about having to continually hang around in lobbies waiting for Andy and me.

"Every time, Henry. Every time. It's either McCoy who's late or... Oh, here he comes now!" complained Seamus.

"I'll speak to 'em."

Paul added, "Yeah, we're fuckin' sick of it."

Seamus and Paul. Despite the amount of time we had spent together at that point, I'd still not fully worked out those two. Paul, with his New York street smarts, in some ways was the easier of the two to get on with. His degree of affability, though, changed from day to day and, during difficult parts of the touring experience, from hour to hour, degenerating at times into downright hostility. It was because of these dramatic mood swings that I suspected at the time that he was a regular user of cocaine. Despite my witnessing Paul's predilection for the nose candy, I later found out this was not the case. It was just Paul.

Now, Seamus was another kind of mystery. A fellow Londoner with a dry sense of humour and a ready wit, Seamus would also make an occasional stab at camaraderie. But there was also a tangible element of aloofness, of holding back, in his attitude towards Andy and I. It was as if Seamus saw us as unwelcome gatecrashers at an exclusive party where, despite his disapproval, he had decided it was best to say nothing as (a) the gate-crashers looked a bit dangerous and (b) it wasn't his party, anyway.

This did fit the facts. Seamus and Paul had both played with Iggy in the past and had contributed to the *Instinct* record thus, having put in the work and paid their dues as passengers on this lucrative world tour.

Andy and I, on the other hand, had stepped into the band from nowhere. At least, I suspected that was Seamus's evaluation. Again, this was a situation outside my experience of band politics, but what I *did* know was that things could change. Comradeship, if not friendship, could still be forged, and a mutual respect achieved. It was just that we were not there yet.

Iggy limped into view from the hotel coffee shop with Suchi following behind. He gave me the briefest nod of recognition before he slumped into an armchair in a corner of the lobby looking tired and drawn.

We had played 23 shows since our Texas Stadium appearance, and our Mr Osterberg was beginning to pay a harsh physical price for the fearless athleticism of his wild twin, Mr Pop. He had pulled a thigh muscle, had a gash across his left eye, a deep wound to his chest plus a whole bunch of painful bumps and bruises that covered his entire body. It was only after Iggy had left the stage and the adrenalin had subsided that he became aware of the injuries collected when hurling himself through the drum kit, or falling off an amplifier, or by letting some demented chick in the front row take chunks out of his flesh with her sharpened nails.

Then, in the dressing room, after the decompression was complete, he would become aware of what he had done to himself, or of what he had allowed to be done, and the mot du jour would be 'angst'. Close to tears, inconsolable, a 41 year old man unable to prevent the inevitable painful rock 'n' roll stigmata accumulated night after night during his trance-like states.

There was one particular night in Austin, Texas, when Iggy passed a stage-hand post-gig covered in blood from a head wound and black and blue from diving off the drum riser into the wiremesh-covered monitors. As Iggy sauntered by, dripping vital fluids, the stage-hand shouted, "How goes the war?"

Without breaking stride, Iggy answered, "Can't you see…? The bad guys are winning."

The bad guys were winning alright and there were no signs to an end to that particular war. But there again, Iggy Pop was never one to go gently into that good night.

Thirty minutes had passed since I'd arrived in the lobby and we still hadn't moved. Iggy was getting agitated.

"Henry, why're we still sitting here?"

"It's Andy, Jim. I phoned him a half-dozen times now. He keeps saying he'll be right down and then doesn't turn up."

Iggy had the solution.

"You go drag his ass down here while the rest of us get on the bus, okay?"

I knew why Andy was late, why Andy was always late. While the rest of us had a medium-sized suitcase and one, at most two pieces of hand luggage, he wasn't one for travelling light. The hugest pair of suitcases you'd ever seen, filled to bursting point with cowboy boots, leather trousers, jackets, shirts, waistcoats with corresponding numerous over-stuffed small bags and a collection of plastic duty free types containing his magazines and rubbish. Also, while most of the band packed their suitcases the night before, ready for a quick getaway the following morning, Andy's road etiquette consisted of leaving all his packing until Henry was hammering on his hotel door with threats of redundancy.

On the big bus with driver Jim revving up the engine, at least we felt we had made some progress. Iggy went to the back room to rest, with Suchi in attendance, while I staked myself out a seat by the window across from the still grumbling Seamus and Paul. Henry appeared and climbed aboard.

"Okay, relax. He's coming." A short while later, Andy emerged through the hotel doors followed by a puffing red-faced porter dragging a trolley loaded with Andy's ponderous suitcases, and his vast collection of assorted bags.

Standing sentry at the hotel entrance stood a black, overweight, uniformed doorman. A man no doubt used to opening and closing doors for awkward-fitting middle class suits and holiday-makers in polyester leisure wear.

Now, out of the corner of his eye, Andy had come into view wearing plumage of a very different kind. For today's little drive from Orlando to Miami, McCoy had decided on a combination that went as follows:

- One widebrimmed velvet hat with blue and gold satin headscarf underneath.
- One green velvet, silver tasselled waistcoat over white whisky-stained woman's blouse with red embroidered flower motif.
- One pair of gold tight-fitting lamé pants partially covered by black patent leather chaps under wide gold-buckled red leather belt.
- One pair of alligator cowboy boots complete with silver spurs held on by studded leather straps that spelled (naturally) the name 'Andy' on one shoe and 'McCoy' on the other.
- One pair Middle Eastern style silver and turquoise heavy earrings, a collection of bracelets running up both arms, all topped off by a fake leopard-skin coat worn casually over his skinny shoulders like some European film director.

As this six foot, colourful vision loped by, the doorman did a quick double-take. It was like a scene from a *Roadrunner* cartoon where Willie Coyote's head turns one way, but his eyes emerge from their sockets on stalks and take off in the opposite direction in disbelief at what they have just seen. The doorman took a second glance, his jaw dropped and the look that followed read, 'What the motherfuckin' Hell was that?' Oblivious, Andy continued his grand exit from hotel to bus. I called out to Henry, "Quick! Get over here. Check this out!" Henry joined me at the window and together we watched as the doorman's expression quickly changed from disbelief to uncontrollable mirth.

Placing his hands on his big stomach and rolling his eyes skywards, he released a series of staccato belly laughs with a voice like oil and treacle. "Ha ha ha!!! Ha Ha HA HA!" Then shook his head and laughed some more 'til he looked fit to bust, and he was forced to grab the hotel door for support. With tears of incredulity plainly visible in his bright eyes he let out another machine gun round of, "Ha ha ha! Ha Ha HA HA!!!" Henry and I couldn't but help join in with the doorman's infectious laughter. Having caught on to the situation, even Seamus and Paul who, moments before had faces of granite, joined us at the bus window with grins from ear to ear. You would have needed a heart of stone not to laugh.

With Andy finally on the bus, big Jim Boatman drove us out of the hotel forecourt and got us on the highway for our ride across the Florida state.

God, I hate Florida.

Flat, humid place full of Coke-guzzling fat holidaymakers and their stupid fat families. Retirement home internees, spring break high school knuckleheads, nigger-hating, faggot-hating, Jew-hating, spick-hating rednecks. And what's more, Nigel Mansell lives there.

Actually, it's not *that* bad...

It's just that every time I go to Florida, I seem to come across at least one of the species of fucker listed above except not, so far, Nigel Mansell, so I ought to be grateful for small mercies.

As time drifted by, I got fed up with the uneventful scenery and climbed into one of the bus bunks to relax and get a fix on where we had been and what was to come. I turned on the reading light and looked through my diary, full of its tales of pleasure and woe.

It had been a long campaign alright. Fifty-four days travelling the length and breadth of North America.

Monday 26 September – Madison

From Beertown, Milwaukee to the capital of Wisconsin, Madison. Roll up onto the University of Wisconsin campus and realise we've come to an all-American, clean cut, hygienic kind of place. We hate it. Iggy, Andy and I take a walk after soundcheck to sit by a nearby lake and watch the healthy, clean-living students jog by, with big smiles on their smug oatmeal faces.

When the three of us come into view, they take a half mile detour and I swear I even see one of the little darlings cross herself as she dashes by complete with a 'Devil's Disciples At 9 O'Clock, Take Evasive Action', look in her baby blues.

One adventurous chick with, as Iggy points out later, nice tits, world-class legs and a dog-turd for a brain, decides to curtail her exercise to try to make friends with the weird-looking strangers.

"Did you guys know that's the lake that Otis Redding died in?"

"Really?" Iggy says. "Otis's plane crashed here?"

"Yeah. Right over there," she says.

We sit and look at the water for a moment before I say to her, "How sad."

"Not really," she says. "It's now Madison's biggest tourist attraction."

Eat at the hotel. Shuteye. Back on the bus for show-time. About to enter the venue through a back door when some grinning jock student shouts at Iggy, "Where did you get that wig from, freak?" Before Henry and Jos can intervene, Iggy knocks the meat-head down with a classic right hook and stands over him screaming, "Get up, motherfucker... Come on... get up!"

A bunch of the jock's muscle-bound friends square up to us and it looks like we're on for an old fashioned fist fight. Quite disappointed when the university security turn up and put a stop to it. The socked jock was moaning about assault and suchlike so I walk up to him and say, "That's the price of a university education, mate," and try to get in another punch. Jos pulls me away and we go on to play a fierce, aggressive, take-no-prisoners kind of show to an audience that proves that not all members of this campus are assholes.

While we're on the fisticuffs stories, there was another little incident in San Diego. This involved Jos and a certain member of the British group, the Jesus

Seamus and Iggy

and Mary Chain, who replaced the fab Jane's Addiction as support band mid-way through the North American tour.

At soundcheck, I passed them backstage, smiled and gave them a cheery, "Hello." What came back were blank faces and plenty of attitude so I had them figured out as self-important stuffed capons straightaway.

On stage, during their 'check, as they fiddled about with their instruments with as much post-modernist irony as possible, Jos spotted that one of them was smoking a cigarette. Now Iggy had a specially constructed, synthetic, expensive floor surface for dancing on which the crew carefully laid out for each show. To prevent damage to it, a smoking ban had been implemented at soundchecks and show-times with Henry going out of his way to make sure that support bands were aware of this.

This particular band, though, seemed to have decided that because they were one of the British music press's pet groups that they were above such petty laws. Jos was forced to explain for a second time why the cigarette should be smoked offstage. As Jos finished his plea for a little co-operation, the smoking Mary Chain held up his fag to Jos's face, dropped it on the dance surface, letting it burn a little before putting it out with the heel of his boot.

Bang! Thud!

Jos had nutted him and the super cool smoker hit the deck with his ass and hopelessly failed to maintain his King Dick image with blood running from his nose and a ready-to-ruck Yorkshireman bearing down on him. Strangely enough, for the rest of their gigs with us, Jesus and Mary Chain remembered to leave both their cigarettes and their arrogance behind in the dressing room.

Back to the diary:

Monday 3 October – Vancouver

Cool, Canadian town. A room with a view at the Ming Court Hotel. Chinese food, soundcheck, share a joint and beer in Andy's room before show-time. Venue, the Expo Theatre, filled to the brim and band excel in music and movement. Guitarist Billy from The Cult joins us for 'Dog' and we finish off with an on-the-spot version of 'Train Kept A-rollin' ' with Iggy screwing up all the words. Doesn't matter, though. Crowd go nuts anyway. We hear them screaming for more, from our dressing room two blocks away. Post-show, Iggy goes off to do a voice-over on a track for The Cult's new record, tentatively titled *Sonic Temple,* at a studio across town. Andy, Paul and I go to see a band recommended to us called Skinny Puppy. Well, Skinny Puppy were truly fucking awful but backstage (an Iggy Pop tour pass can work wonders) the lead singer of Puppy pulls out a bag of magic mushrooms and says, "Go ahead, have a couple." As sharp as a whip, Andy grabs the whole bag out of his hand and the three of us gulp them down before anyone can stop us. Magnanimous as ever, Andy says, "Thanks for the mushrooms, man... And, by the way, your band sucks!" Laughing hysterically, we do a runner out of the dressing room and onto the street. Hail a cab and back to the zing, bing, ving or what-the-fuck Court Hotel for yet more drug-induced fun.

What I didn't write in my diary entry was that the full psychedelic force of those mushrooms kicked in shortly after the three of us got into that cab. One minute the cabbie was letting three seemingly sane if unconventionally dressed young men into his vehicle, their conversation rational. Next minute, the one with the hat was standing on his seat shouting, "Hey! Turn this pimp faced, whips 'n' furs, wise-assed pussy mobile around so I can get some of those things that give off smoke and make your belly sound like coffee... Please." All while the feisty New Yorker and the dude with the English accent point at the saliva dripping from the hat guy's mouth and laugh manically.

Yeah, that poor bastard had a frozen smile to his face all the way back to our hotel. He was certain that he had let in three murderously psychotic escaped lunatics and it would be an act of God if he made it through the ride without injury

His prayers .vere answered, though, and even in the state I was in I couldn't help but feel sorry for this frightened cabbie and gave him a $50 tip. This seemed to please him, not surprisingly as it was a $6 ride. He produced a genuine smile before screeching off in his cab at what Paul estimated to be at least 75 miles an hour. Andy, Paul and I stood a while waving him off. Then, putting on our best psycho-terrorist faces, we ran

Marx Brothers style into the Ming Court's bar, becoming the worst nightmare of a bunch of grey-suited conservative businessmen.

Henry's head pushed through my bunk curtains, and in his top Caledonian accent he informed me, "We're in Miami, sonny boy... You know that show *Miami Vice?* Well, if it's anything like that, you and your mate Andy will be in hog heaven."

Later, I looked on this comment as a kind of prophesy.

MIAMI LICE

Now, I won't bore you with the details of our Miami show. Suffice to say that our gig at the downtown 4,000 seat Cameo Theatre was one of the finest of the whole world tour. The really interesting stuff, though, happened after our performance and I figure we best get to it...

After having played our final encore, we headed back to the dressing room with Iggy going into his, "Did they like me? Did they hate me? Am I crazy?" spiel. This had become something of a fixture to this second American tour.

Having dutifully answered, "What d'you mean? You were great, Jim. They loved us!" and suchlike, he started to calm down. A couple of hits of a joint and a glass of wine later and Iggy was relaxed, happy and asking the promoter what was on for that night. The promoter rubbed his hands with glee and informed us that a couple of limos were waiting outside to whisk us off to Club New where the Iggy Pop-adoring club owner had laid on some free food, champagne and much more besides.

"Perfect," we said. Nothing like a spot of nightclubbing, with the owner picking up the tab, to lift the spirits of a road-weary band.

On arriving at the club, the hand-shaking, sharp-suited owner led us proudly to the cordoned-off VIP area.

Cool.

This place was a classic. An exact replica of what would be my fantasy Miami nightclub. A dance floor with small-waisted over-dressed Cuban girls gyrating and dry-humping to the sounds of the Miami Sound Machine and 70s disco, their super-cool boyfriends posing and preening nearby in the club's full-length mirrors, high-cheekboned and real handsome. Latinos with slicked-back ponytailed hair the colour of night, dressed to kill in their razor-sharp suits and Massimo Livio Italian silk ties.

The decor of the place was bad Art Deco. A tasteless, black-gold and mirrored attempt at a 1930s Fred Astaire and Ginger Rogers movie set. On the subject of movies, if any of you have seen the movie *Carlito's Way*, then conjure up the club run by Al Pacino in that film and you'll have a perfect idea of what this place was like. At a snap of the owner's fingers, ice buckets containing good champagne were brought to our tables, and menus placed in our hands by pretty hostesses in low-cut tight-fitting cocktail dresses. None of us were hungry, so we just guzzled down the champagne and admired the view.

I noticed Andy had made friends with a long-limbed girl with claims to a professional modelling career. Together they left their seats and disappeared into the VIP toilets; my first thought was that the horny bastard was going for a stand-up screw in one of the cubicles. Then I remembered what Miami is famous for – a once popular TV series starring Don Johnson, its Art Deco architecture, its pink flamingos. And, for those who have an interest in that kind of thing – its cocaine.

And, sure enough, on entering the toilet, there was Andy with one end of a straw up his nose and the other end in a huge bag filled to the top with Charlie.

The girl gestured for me to join in, and after Andy had finished hoovering up a large portion, I grabbed the straw off him and took a snort. It was face-freezing, gum-numbing, high quality cocaine and as I dived in for seconds, Iggy walked in on us.

"What are you two rock 'n' roll fuckers up to?"

I guess the straw up my nose was the give-away.

Iggy walked over, looked in the bag and said, "Cool. Can I have some?"

What? Iggy on coke…? Well, I guess if he was going to fuck up on this tour, Miami was the place to do it.

Looking back over his shoulder to check no-one was coming in, Iggy snorted up a man-sized portion.

"Mmmm… That's good shit…" Sniff, sniff… "Mighty fine!"

Then it was back to the tables for more champagne, and a look of pure innocence from Iggy in reply to Suchi's enquiring expression.

"Jim, you've got white stuff on your nose."

"Have I honey? Oh, well, I'll make sure to get all the soap off the next time I wash my face in the bathroom."

Come 3am, all attempts at restraint and concealment had been abandoned. Coke dealers were coming up handing us free gram bags first, shaking hands and telling us their names second. We were doing lines off the marble table tops in full view of the Cuban regulars on the dance floor, who would look at us, pull bags of snow out of their top pockets and shout, "Miami coke, eez good sheet, right?"

To which we would truthfully reply, "Fuckin' A."

We were doing it directly out of bags, sprinkling it on wine, giving it away to hostesses as tips.

By this time, Iggy was totally wired. Quivering bottom lip, rapid-fire speech pattern, and a look of 'I want more, more, more' on his face.

A bunch of shapely women descended upon us, attracted by the champagne, snow and rock stars. One particularly nice piece of eye-candy sat down next to me and introduced herself. She was low temperature; Scandinavian, blonde hair, clear blue eyes. An ice queen beauty. Before ten seconds were up, the ice had melted. She'd taken my champagne glass out of my hand and planted her red lips on mine. I couldn't have stopped her even if I'd wanted to, being, by that time, too fucked up on wine and stutter dust.

She wanted to jump my train, but I derailed that manoeuvre when she pulled out of my pocket a gram zip-locked bag and proceeded to vacuum clean up the contents with her nose. Ultimately, she was after one thing, and I decided that I wanted no dealings with a coke slut.

"Henry, I'm off," I shouted across the room before I staggered out of the club and into a waiting white limo.

Seconds later, Iggy and Andy jumped in and we drove off in the direction of our hotel. We hadn't driven more than two blocks before Iggy pulled out a bag from his leather jacket containing what I guessed to be about ten grams of Charlie.

"Oh, fuck," I screamed. "Not more of the stuff... Ain't you two had enough?"

Apparently not. With manic glee, they both set about the contents of the bag with straws, and had hoovered up a good amount of it by the time we stepped into the hotel lobby. The girl Andy had met at the club had followed the limo in her car and, arm in arm, she and Andy took off for his room.

Iggy wanted to do stuff, "Hey, Alvin, let's go swimming or get out the guitars and play a bit or..."

As he continued with his list of things to do, I noticed that Iggy couldn't stand still. He was jerking his arms around, grinding his teeth and doing what looked like a kind of soft-shoe-shuffle on the spot.

Generally, cocaine affects people in one of two ways. There are the symptoms that Iggy was exhibiting: hyperactiveness; sweats; lip-biting and super-tense facial contortions. Or, there's my reaction: a belief that I am the most articulate man in the world, resulting in a five hour dissertation on any given subject; a quadrupling of my capacity for alcohol, which at that time was considerable anyway and, finally, a display of laid-back behaviour so extreme that friends have been known to check my pulse.

Two incompatible reactions to the same drug.

"No, Jim," I said, "I don't really fancy any of that. I'm going to my room to find some non-interruptive music on the radio and drink some of my cognac 'til sleep comes down."

Iggy looked disappointed but understood. As I waited for the elevator, a thought occurred.

"Jim, where's Suchi?"

"She's on her way with Henry in another limo... Hey, maybe she'll want to go swimming?"

An hour later, there was a desperate hammering at my door. I looked through the hotel room spy-hole, one of those kind that gives you a fish-eye

lens perspective, and there were Iggy's distorted features looking back at me. He looked not unlike the angst-ridden figure on the bridge in the Edvard Munch painting *The Scream*. My God! I thought, he looks terrible. I unbolted the door and let him in.

Iggy came storming into my room dressed only in underwear, wild-eyed and frantic.

"Quick, Alvin, give me a brandy. I'm going fuckin' nuts!"

"Sure," I said. "Sit down."

"I can't sit down, man... I've been marching up and down my room for an hour now. It's driving Suchi crazy. It's like I've got fuckin' lice in my pants."

I poured a large amount of cognac into a glass and handed it to him. Iggy quickly gulped it down and asked for another. "I'm so damn wired... Got to calm down... Hey, let's go see Andy."

So we did.

Iggy, still in his underwear, me in just a pair of old jeans with the ass hanging out, banging on Andy's door at 5am. McCoy seemed pleased to see us. I think the litre bottle of Martell I was holding had something to do with his unexpected, generous response. When we got into his room, I noticed that Andy was in his underwear too. Sprawled out on his couch, completely naked but utterly comfortable with our presence, the girl from the club was smoking a large joint.

"Hi, guys... Come join the party."

Iggy spotted the joint and whisked it out of her hand.

"Just what I needed... Fuckin' yeah... this is helping."

We played guitars, wrote songs which we forgot almost directly after their composition, and told stories, with the naked girl pouring us brandies and rolling us joints until the sun came up. By 7am, I was ready for sleep and got up to leave. Andy was ready for his bed and said so. Iggy had no choice but to walk back up the corridor with me to his room. He still seemed agitated, with his breathing close to hyperventilation, but there was not much more I could do for him.

"Here, Jim. Take the rest of this cognac. You look like you might need it."

He took the bottle and said, "Listen, man, when I get in my room, if I'm still driving Suchi mad with my pacing and sleeplessness, can I come back and watch TV or something?"

"Yeah," I said. "If it's still bad, just knock."

"Thanks, Alvin."

With that, he made for his room and didn't come back.

In my seven months of touring with him, that was the only time I ever saw Iggy fuck up. Before and after Miami, he drank moderately, kept to sharing one or two joints after shows, and left his big hits and highs for on-stage only. He would even tell the audience about it each night before we played 'High On You'.

"You know, in the past, I used to get fucked up on drugs and booze until I didn't even know who the fuck I was anymore. But now, I've swapped that shit for a different high... I'm getting high on my music... On my band... I'm getting real fuckin' high on you"

Everyone is due one moment of misjudgement and madness on a long rock 'n' roll tour. That moment when you swim out on a sea of enthusiasm and eagerness only to suddenly find that you're out of your depth and sinking fast.

Andy's moment came in New York, Iggy's was in Miami, and mine...? Well, mine was yet to come.

BAD MEDICINE

Another continent. Another time change. My watch reads 10am and I've entered the arena of the unwell.

Coughing and spluttering the whole drive from Amsterdam airport to our hotel in the city centre, and silently cursing the bastard I'd caught the flu germs from. Towards the end of the North American tour, just about every member of the touring party had come down with some illness or other. A natural consequence of the gruelling schedule, late nights and international foolishness involved in crossing the North American continent.

But in other ways, the band had become much stronger. We had come through what everyone agreed was the toughest part of the world tour so far. We were meaner, leaner, with rock-hard musical muscles. We were ready for anything, believing our 20 date dash around Europe would be a breeze.

As we drove into Amsterdam on that frosty November morning, we already had two Euro shows under our belts. A feisty gig in to a spunky, spiky crowd of Deutschlanders and a sedate affair in Ghent, Belgium with an interesting pre-gig occurrence.

Our hotel in Ghent was a Holiday Inn which stood alongside a busy, noisy motorway on the outskirts of the town. We had arrived the night before the actual show and, heavily jet-lagged and unable to sleep, I was, for once, glad to pick up the ringing bedside telephone at 8am.

It was Andy.

"Alvin. Cool, you're up."

"Yeah, Andy. Couldn't sleep... Jet-lagged and restless."

"Right. Meet me down in the bar in five minutes for a breakfast beer. I've been down there and the Everly Brothers' band are sat around drinking coffee... And you know how much I dig the Everly Brothers..."

Well, I didn't actually. I hadn't really pegged Andy down as a fan of slick, clean-cut Phil and Don and material like 'Cathy's Clown'. But I had come to understand that, although Andy was the type of guy who gets carried *into*

bars for an evening's drinking, he also had a sentimental side to his nature which occasionally surfaced in these sorts of disclosures.

As I arrived at the bar, Andy was supping on a glass of beer and talking to a stocky American.

"Alvin, man, you gotta talk to this guy, he's played with Elvis!"

The stocky American turned out to be the drummer for the Everly Brothers touring band and indeed at one time he had hit the skins for The King in the early 70s. He was just about to finish a story, set in Las Vegas, about Elvis, Tom Jones and some horny chick, when in walked Phil Everly. Andy shot out of his chair and didn't waste any time.

"Hey, you're Phil Everly, right?"

"Yessir, that's me."

Phil was a bona fide nice bloke with a cool smile and seemed as ego-free as any musician can possibly be. I got him a cup of coffee and he told us how his tour was progressing. He genuinely seemed pleased to communicate with a couple of fellow touring musicians. But Andy wanted more.

"Phil, where's that brother of yours?"

"Oh, Don's still up in his room. He doesn't usually come down until the last possible moment, and there's still 30 minutes to setting off time."

Andy was persistent.

"Gimme his room number so I can go up and say hello. You know it would be such a thrill to tell people that I met both the Everly Brothers in person."

Phil declined.

"Well, you know, that's not such a good idea. See, Don really likes his privacy and you've got to respect that, right...?"

With all the sincerity that he could muster, Andy replied, "Of course, man... I respect that."

No more than two minutes later, Andy was in the lobby telling the desk clerk a pack of lies.

"Yeah... Phil Everly has asked me to go up and tell his brother Don that the band's ready to leave and I'm gonna help with his guitars and stuff... And, thing is, I've forgotten his room number."

The desk clerk looked at us, figured we seemed like guys who either worked with, or played in, a band and after checking the rooming list on the VDU, said, "Mr Don Everly is in room 373."

In the elevator on the way up to the third floor, I tried to talk Andy out of what he had in mind.

"Come on, man... You've heard what Phil said. The man's a virtual recluse. He's famed for it... He's the Howard Hughes of two-part harmonies."

This had no effect on McCoy whatsoever, so, when we got within two doors of room 373, I grabbed him by the shoulders and asked him to reconsider.

"Andy, look, his door's open. You can't just walk in on the man like this... He may get violent."

There was a typical McCoy response. "Oh, fucking Hell... Don't be such a pussy. Don Everly is my hero... He'll be pleased to see me."

And sure enough, while I maintained my two room distance from 373, Andy marched up and walked through the open door. Though I couldn't see what went down, I heard every word of the conversation.

"Hi, Don. My name is Andy McCoy and I'm..."

"Who the fuck are you?"

"I'm a fan of yours, man."

"I don't give a shit who you are. You're leaving my room NOW!"

"Oh, come on, don't..."

"You don't enter a man's room just like that without even knocking on his door. Out before I throw you out!"

Andy tried to explain, "Listen, you got it wrong, I..."

"I told you... OUT!!"

Andy came flying out of the room backwards, and landed on his ass on the corridor carpet as Don's room door slammed shut after him. I helped Andy to his feet and just about managed not to say, "I fuckin' told you so."

Andy pulled himself together, dusted himself down and straightened his hat. As we walked back down the corridor, he turned to me and, without a hint of irony in his voice whatsoever, said, "I always thought Don Everly was a cunt."

*

Our hotel in Amsterdam was a modern, smoked glass and chrome affair, complete with those annoying synthetic carpets that create static electricity, so that every time you touch a door handle or something metallic, you receive a nasty little shock.

Paul, Seamus and Andy decided to take off to a local coffee shop called The Bulldog, to do a particular kind of shopping. Amsterdam has dozens of these coffee shops and bars, their main attraction being that they are openly and legally allowed to sell marijuana and hashish over their counters, along with the beers and cappuccino.

Feeling tired and weak from the flu, I declined to join them and, instead, sat in on a series of interviews which Iggy was giving the Euro Press in the hotel's conference room; the main appeal for me being the endless supplies of fresh orange juice and hot coffee served by a hotel waiter.

I also found it real interesting to observe Iggy in this situation, handling his interrogators with skill and consummate ease. As I sat sipping the OJ and chewing on vitamin pills, I listened to Iggy patiently telling his life story for the thousandth time to some Parisian hack who hadn't even done the most basic research on his subject.

Iggy told him he was born James Newell Osterberg Jr, in the spring of 1947 in the resort town of Muskegon on the eastern shore of Lake Michigan. He had spent his childhood years living in Ann Arbor and Ypsilanti trailer parks, his father a teacher, his mother a housewife.

"...I was a studious kid at school, an avid reader and academically adept... I always seemed to get good grades."

After graduating from high school in 1965, Iggy spent a semester studying anthropology at the University of Michigan before deciding that his future lay in a different direction. He had been the hard-hitting drummer of his high school band, The Iguanas, and it was during that time that he acquired the nickname Iggy and a desire to become a professional musician.

"...Yeah, I was hooked. But while the other guys in The Iguanas dug Beatles songs, I was really into The Rolling Stones, The Kinks and the blues legends like Howlin' Wolf and Muddy Waters. So I looked around for something else."

Iggy swapped a university education for a job in an Ann Arbor record store, quit The Iguanas and joined a local white blues band, The Prime Movers. Through beating the skins for the Movers, Iggy was introduced to a pool of enthusiastic musicians in the Ann Arbor music scene. These included Wayne Kramer, who went on to make a fine noise with the legendary Detroit band The MC5, and Ron and Scott Ashton who would feature heavily in Iggy's future musical endeavours.

Iggy also played the occasional sit-in gig with visiting Detroit-based Motown groups like The Four Tops and The Shangri-Las. From his vantage point on the drum stool, he learned the importance of stage presentation from these slick Motown professionals.

By 1966, Iggy was heavily into R & B music and, after quitting The Prime Movers, he moved to Chicago in search of authentic blues music and musicians. When his Chicago sojourn failed to yield up the secrets of the blues, he returned to his hometown, phoned the Ashton Brothers, and in the spring of 1967, together they formed The Stooges.

"...At first we were what you might call an experimental outfit. An instrumental three piece with Ron and Scott on bass and drums and with me playing a loud Hawaiian steel guitar and occasional vacuum cleaner... People thought we were weird."

Only after Iggy had caught a Doors show, featuring a crazed and loaded Jim Morrison playing with his dick and coming on like Baudelaire on speed, did he decide to make the switch to lead singer. The Morrison performance had been an awakening. It had demonstrated to Iggy that the stage could effectively be used by a skilled and fearless front man as a place for psychic exploration and erotic, dramatic self-expression. With every intention of following in the Lizard King's footsteps, Iggy got Ron Ashton to switch to guitar and recruited local boy Dave Alexander on bass.

This left Iggy free to blow minds across the state of Michigan, with some of the most intense, shocking and brilliant performances any audience had witnessed from a singer on a rock 'n' roll stage. From their first show with this line up in March 1968, they attracted a twisted but addicted following and sensational press coverage. Just seven months later that same year, they found themselves signed to Elektra Records.

The following two years saw the recording and release of their self-titled debut record *The Stooges* and the follow-up, *Funhouse*. These are two of the finest collections of napalm-hearted in-your-face rock 'n' roll songs ever committed to vinyl. Each composition a venom-laced dark piece of chocolate. These records were the antithesis of the laid-back, acid-influenced vibe of the popular West Coast sound of the time. This music talked of violence, boredom, sexuality, riots and war. It spoke of trash culture, the TV generation, terrorism and nihilism.

Instead of wasting their time on writing some immature, Utopian, peace 'n' love fantasy or a wigged-out, LSD-inspired travelogue, Iggy and The Stooges focused on the real experiences of Middle American youth. In the terminology of the time, they were a 'heavy trip'.

From 1964 to 1974, the Vietnam war was being waged. Iggy beat the draft by beating his meat and acting like a drooling maniac in front of the draft board. He may have escaped the fire fights and napalm nightmares of South East Asia, but during the touring for *Funhouse,* he discovered another kind of Charlie in the chemical jungle, and slipped into a grim, drug-induced Hell.

"...I remember one party back when I lived in LA with The Stooges. I woke up on a couch with people around me and felt a terrible pain in my left leg. Looking down, I saw the cigarette I'd been holding had burned a half inch hole in my thigh, with smoke and the smell of burning flesh and everything. But I was too fucked up to care and those around me were too

fucked up to notice... So I went back to sleep."

It was during this period of drugs and disintegration that Elektra dropped the band and Iggy met Bowie. With Bowie's help, The Stooges went on to make one more record for CBS, *Raw Power* before the substance abuse and Iggy's unsustainable close-to-the-edge lifestyle led to the final break-up of the band.

Iggy committed himself to an LA psychiatric institution.

"...Yeah, I was gone. That place straightened me out and gave me the ability to deal with my life again."

After leaving hospital, Iggy recorded what I believe to be one of his most under-rated albums, *Kill City,* with guitarist James Williamson, in the spring of 1975. This was followed by the critically-acclaimed, Bowie-produced *The Idiot* and *Lust for Life,* both released in 1977 during his Berlin years.

By this time, Iggy had become a new wave icon. His career was on the up and with the release of the excellent *New Values* in 1979. All the top faces of the UK punk rock scene were paying homage to him, covering his music and citing him as a major influence. A few of them, like long-time fans Brian James of The Damned and Glen Matlock of The Sex Pistols even got to play with him.

But with the advent of the 80s, Iggy lost momentum, with what were, for me, three very disappointing records, *Soldier* (1980), *Party* (1981) and *Zombie Birdhouse* (1982). I think the fact that Iggy didn't even consider one song from any of these three albums for inclusion in our Instinct set-list speaks for itself.

During this period, he also fell back into his hedonistic, wanton ways. Back on the juice, back on the hard drugs and anything-with-a-pulse-will-do pussy patrol, with the quality of his life fast diminishing.

He reached crisis point in 1983 and, once again, sought out professional help in Los Angeles, going through a detoxification programme at a live-in clinic. Slowly, he was able to make order out of chaos. Meeting his future wife Suchi during a Japanese tour that same year provided a big impetus.

With the desire to change strong in him, Iggy embarked on a programme of self-improvement and in the process managed to shed his old skin. With news of the new, improved, better-with-age Iggy Pop came a record deal with A&M and the recording of his most accessible and commercial album to date, *Blah Blah Blah.*

"...Yeah, it was my best selling album ever. Even had a hit single from it, 'Real Wild Child', which I was very pleased about. I'm hoping *Instinct* can do even better, though."

It was an amazing tale.

As I finished my eighth orange juice and watched Iggy shake hands with the Parisian penpusher, the drama of his story had me thinking that what I had just heard was nothing less than a modern day rock 'n' roll *Iliad*.

Soon after, I left for my room, to find Andy standing outside my hotel door wrapping away with his knuckles.

"Hey, McCoy, what you been up to?"

"Oh, Alvin, there you are. I've gone and bought you something for your flu."

"Really? That's kind... Let's go inside."

No sooner had we got through the door before Andy pulled out a clear plastic ziplock bag with something that looked like a large rabbit's turd in it. He started flapping it in front of my face with a big grin on his saying, "Nepalese hash, man... The finest in the world. This will make you feel a whole lot better."

"Andy, I'm not sure if that's the kind of medicine I need," I said.

Andy was adamant.

"Nonsense. You must listen to Dr McCoy... Trust me!"

With that he broke off a piece of the rabbit's turd and handed it to me.

"Swallow."

"Look, Andy, I really..."

"Swallow!!"

There are times when Andy can catch a person at a moment of weakness. A moment when you actually believe his intentions are pure and his judgement trustworthy. This, unfortunately, was just such a moment.

I popped the hash into my mouth and swallowed. Andy also broke himself off a piece and ate it. For 20 minutes or so, I listened to how he, Paul and Seamus had haggled with the guy in The Bulldog for the best deal on their hash. How he was going to use his new Stratocaster guitar at the show tonight, how he...

I began to feel decidedly strange.

"Listen, Andy, this is all very interesting but is it me or is there a distinct echo in this room?"

Andy's reply confirmed my worst fears, "What (what-what-what...) are (are-are-are...) you (you-you-you...)?"

I got off my chair with the intention of walking to the window to get some air, and found the floor had turned to quicksand. I seemed to sink deeper and deeper with each successive step. Oh, shit... I was in the Fear Zone.

There was a knock at the door and Andy jumped up and answered it. It was Henry.

"What are you twos up to (to-to-to...)?"

I looked round at him from my spot in the quicksand and gave a weak smile. He continued, "Down in the lobby in five minutes (five minutes-five minutes-five minutes...) and I mean five minutes (five minutes-five minutes-five minutes...) and don't be late (late-late-late...)."

The soundcheck was a Dante-esque experience. A certified, 100% bona fide nightmare. The venue, The Paradiso was a converted church with a dome roof and an upper balcony, a place of past triumphs for the UK Subs. Under normal conditions, this would have been a gig I'd have looked forward to playing. But as the Nepalese hash kicked in harder and harder, I feared this could be my last show. Being sent home in disgrace, seemed a likely outcome of taking trusty Dr McCoy's advice. During the soundcheck numbers, the echo effect got stronger and more and more exaggerated 'til at one point I couldn't even work out what song we were supposed to be playing, let alone my part in it. Paul and Seamus were giving me quizzical looks, so I decided to tell them that the flu had affected my hearing and I'd better sit out the rest of the 'check. That's what I intended to say, but when I opened my mouth, they were forced to listen to the gibberish and ravings of a man in the grip of severe hashish poisoning. Andy covered for me.

"Shit man, your flu *is* bad... You sound delirious. I'll get Henry to drive you back to the hotel."

The only good thing about that soundcheck was that Iggy failed to turn up due to some added interviews. I figured at least I wouldn't be officially fired until after the show that night.

Back at the hotel, I collapsed into my bed and got some sleep. When I awoke, I looked at my watch and saw I'd been in the arms of a dissipated, far out Morpheus for some four hours, and hauled myself up onto the side of the bed. On stepping down onto the floor, I discovered the quicksand had been replaced by cotton wool, but it still took determination to walk in a straight line. Speaking aloud, I found I could now string a coherent sentence together but I was still in the echo chamber (chamber-chamber-chamber...). My words reverberated around my head. It would be touch and go as to whether I could pull it off that night.

Back at The Paradiso, I did my best to appear sane and normal, and flogged the flu angle for all it was worth.

"Really...? I look a bit shaky? Must be this flu, Henry. I'll be fine once we're up there." In a corner of the dressing room, as I practised walking straight, Andy came across to have a chat.

"Man, what's wrong with you today?"

I couldn't contain my anger any longer. "You...! You fucker...! That's what's wrong with me. You poisoned me with that so-called Nepalese medicine of yours. If I mess up this gig because of it, and end up getting the sack, it'll be your head that'll be knocking off your shoulders before I split. Do you understand?"

Andy was ready for that one.

"Oh, come on. I took as much of that shit as you and I'm fine."

I was ready for that.

"Yeah, that's because you're a fuckin' aberration. A freak of nature! You're the type of abnormal bastard who could swallow a drugstore, wash it down with a vat of whisky, and still be looking around for something stronger."

Paul interrupted our little tête-à-tête with the dread news that it was time to move it out. Like a condemned man on his way to the gallows, I followed the rest of the band out of the dressing room and onto that fateful stage.

During the first two numbers, I was decidedly dodgy. I thought, this is it; Iggy will bludgeon me to death up here with his mike stand, and deadly Dr McCoy will have added another victim to his prodigious list.

But by song three, the tide started to turn. Despite the persistent echo and paranoia (noia-noia-noia...) I hung onto the boom/crack of Paul's kick and snare drums, the essential listening for a bass player, with grim determination, and played along accordingly. On reaching the middle of the set, I took one last look round at the faces of the band to make sure no-one was glaring at me and, thankfully, saw only contented expressions. I realised then that I'd managed to snatch victory from the jaws of defeat and allowed myself the luxury of believing I would make it through this tour after all.

There was no letting up, though. Right up to the very last number, I had to battle the effects of the Nepalese and concentrate on the work at hand.

On returning backstage, I was shattered. Paul came over and put his arm around my shoulder.

"You were great tonight, man. Solid as a rock."

Iggy shouted his agreement from under a towel.

"Yeah, Alvin. You should get sick more often... You played like a motherfucker!"

Despite a valiant attempt to curtail my world-touring, by one Andy McCoy and a certain export from the state of Nepal, I had, in the end, turned in one of my best personal performances.

And, as bizarre as it may seem, I have to admit that my flu symptoms did disappear completely.

Isn't it good to hear a positive drug story for a change?

A CONCISE HISTORY
OF A EUROPEAN TOUR

What follows is a series of day-to-day entries written during the remainder of the Iggy Pop Band 1988 European Winter Tour. They are taken directly from my tour diary and were scrawled down in hotel rooms and aeroplanes in less than ideal conditions: extreme fatigue, alcohol-inspired madness and some kind of nausea being the norms. Still, they provide an accurate picture of events.

Wednesday 9 November – Copenhagen, Denmark
Despite what the song says, Copenhagen is not so wonderful if you are still suffering the effects of an overdose of mind-numbingly strong Nepalese black hash. Straight to my room on arrival at the Sheraton Hotel to shower and sleep. Two English cooks have been added to our tour party. Patsy and Jackie from the rock 'n' roll caterers, Eat to the Beat, have flown over to cook our meals from now on. It was a cold day in Copenhagen, so hot stew followed by bread pudding and custard was served up post-gig. We had decided it would be digestive suicide to eat that kind of fare before a show. As for the show itself… File under cool and groovy. Dash back to the Sheraton and into Iggy's room for the American presidential election results on CNN. Fuck… fuck… fuck… That Republican asshole Bush and his global village idiot running mate li'l Danny Quayle have gone and won the election. My personal belief is that they are spawn of Satan. Be prepared to observe their eyes glowing red at you out of your TV screens any day now.

Thursday 10 November – Oslo, Norway
More flying today, which is cool as there is nothing like a couple of free cocktails served by a pretty stewardess to make the afternoon swing by. Touch down in Oslo and a bit of a drive through the Norwegian snow to the Scandinavia Hotel. This directly faces a palace which one presumes houses the local royals. Thought about knocking

on their door for a cup of sugar but got talked into playing a concert at somewhere called Skedsmohallen. Rolls off the tongue, doesn't it? In my hotel, room 409, the show's been over for a couple of hours but I can't for the life of me remember if it was good or bad. File this one under mystery. Must be that Nepalese hash. Think I'll knock on Andy's door and land the Scandinavian poisoner one on the jaw.

Medicating me, indeed!

Friday 11 November – Stockholm, Sweden

Hour's flight. Blonde Nordic goddess serves us nuts, newspapers and one of those 'who-let-this-rabble-in' looks. Seamus and I wave back at the road crew in economy from our comfortable, roomy business class seats. Henry tells us to behave, and Iggy ends up autographing a million promo photos for Ms Goddess and friends after she learns who he is and suddenly warms to us.

Stockholm's the city Andy McCoy grew up in. I know this 'cos since leaving Oslo this morning, he has told me, the rest of the band and each member of the crew, about 1,000 times each.

Stockholm *is* a wonderful city. Grand and elegant buildings and Age of Reason architecture to rival any capital in Europe. Our hotel, the Grand, is a reflection of all that. Yet again, there's a royal palace, this time across a river.

Dump our gear in our hotel rooms and straight back into the limos for the soundcheck at our venue for the evening, the Solna Hallen.

Decide to risk Patsy's and Jackie's enticing dinner pre-gig tonight as it's fish with winter vegetables and Iggy reckons it won't hinder our movements.

There are still three hours to kill to show-time so back again to the Grand.

Strange developments on our arrival. Out of the limos and about to enter the hotel when armed Swedish police surround us and inform Henry that no-one can enter. Turns out the Vice-President of Iraq is also a guest and there has been a death threat made by some Middle Eastern organisation or other; as a result we will have to wait an hour before we can get in. Madness. Good money has been paid for fine rooms and we are in desperate need of some rest and relaxation. Just as everybody starts their righteous indignation, finger-pointing and raised-voice routines, I spot the solution to our problem. "Hey, fellas, over here." Henry and the band join me round the corner from the main hotel entrance. "Look, a service entrance... Let's sneak in." Henry and Suchi are worried about the consequences of such action. "Suppose there are sharpshooters about...? Anyway, they're bound to have officers guarding the other side of that door." "Not necessarily," I reason. "And anyway, what are they going to do...? Shoot us?" Suchi's concise answer to that is, "Probably."

Still, Iggy, Andy, Paul and Seamus are up for giving it a try, and Captain McCoy of the Booze and Drug-Addled Brain Light Infantry seizes his chance to play terrorist and leads the way. The service entrance leads to a delivery bay by the hotel kitchen. Just in front is a door which Andy carefully opens about a half inch. "Yeah, this leads to the main stairs by the lobby." Henry's still worried. "Is there any police about, Andy?" "Yes, there's a geezer with a big fuckin' machine gun by the lift and a bunch of pigs surrounding the entrance but if we're quick and silent, we could make it up the stairs to our rooms without them knowing." "Quick and silent...? Andy, you've been reading too many fucking spy novels again," I say. No answer. Andy is too wrapped up in his movie to listen to that kind of treacherous talk. "Okay... Now!" On Andy's signal we make our dash for the stairs and in jig time we're back in our rooms.

Some bloody security these Swedes have got. I must send a note to Salman Rushdie. "Don't ever go to Stockholm. The security's crap and you'll end up as dog food."

Saturday 12 November – Gothenburg, Sweden

After the excitement of yesterday's 'Iggy Pop band versus the Swedish secret service', and the stunning show that followed, I was quite expecting a very run-of-the-mill kind of day here in Gothenburg. No such thing. A splendid show at the Scandinavian Arena with Iggy as the human rock whirlwind.

Back to the hotel bar with Iggy, Andy and Seamus for a fine cognac, thankfully Iggy picks up the bill as the round sets him back over £100. Just as we are about to head upstairs to Iggy and Suchi's room for a joint and to play around on the guitars, a Swedish nutter by the name of Magnus (honest) comes over to us. Bear-hugging us all individually he says he saw the concert earlier and wants to take us out to visit some happening Gothenburg clubs. Andy, Seamus and I say okay. Iggy, as per usual, is not into nightclubbing, so off the three of us go in Magnus's car.

The man drives like a maniac and we're glad to step out of his BMW alive on reaching a joint in the centre of town. In the club everything is going swimmingly until Andy heads for the bar to get in another round of drinks. He comes back minutes later dripping with booze saying some knuckle-headed yuppie type had just thrown a glass of beer over him and called him scum. Seamus is outraged, "What! Where is the bastard?..." Andy says, "Come on, I'll show you." I get up and follow him, and as I approach the bar, suddenly realise that Seamus is still in his seat and Magnus has disappeared altogether.

Then I spot our beer-dispensing Swedish yuppie... He's huge. Looking like some heavyweight wrestler who has swapped the grappling game for a day job with Saatchi and Saatchi, he is literally bursting out of his designer suit. All of six foot six tall and 300 pounds plus wide. Now, I'm five foot eleven and 150 pounds on a good day, so as we get close to the big bastard I start wondering why the fuck I am doing this. But it's too late to turn back. Andy has shot past me like a demented greyhound, and after delivering a woefully bad attempt at a kick to the guy's balls, announces to the Swedish giant that he is now in for a good kicking from his karate black belt friend.

Well, this is news to me. It's true that I'd studied the martial arts on and off for a couple of years but karate black belt...? Andy is talking utter bollocks. Still, only one way to play it in a situation like this and that's fast and long. "Right, apologise to my friend, give him some money for his dry cleaning bill and buy us both a drink or I'll send you to the nearest hospital." What? Did I say that? This throws the Goliath for a couple of seconds. He looks at me. I stare right back into his eyes and then, looking and sounding ominously like a psychotic Arnold Schwarzenegger, he exercises probably his only two words of English, "Fuck you," and starts towards me. I give him my best shot, an upper cut to the underside of his chin as I can't reach his nose, but it's like Woody Allen trying to deck an LA Raider linebacker. He staggers back a couple of inches, smiles and comes back at me again.

Just as I am about to turn on my heels and run, I see Magnus accompanied by three beefy bouncers running towards us, so I stand my ground. As the thick-necked brute pulls back his fist to land what would have proved a devastating punch to my face, the three bouncers jump on him. Within seconds, they have him pinned on the ground and are kicking the shit out of him. "Don't worry," one of the bouncers says as he lays in his third successive strike to the now semi-conscious bully-boy, "we'll take care of him. Go join your friends and enjoy yourself." Good advice. It has been a close-run thing but McCoy's honour has been restored and I have just about managed to come away with my head still attached to my shoulders. Under the circumstances, we couldn't have hoped for more.

Sunday 13 November – Hamburg, Germany
A late afternoon flight from cold Sweden to cold Germany. Jos gets in his usual hysteria-creating tradition of shouting, "It's just like me dream. We're all going to die!!" Just as the plane reaches lift-off speed and people are nervous enough anyway.

Evening off in Hamburg. Naturally, the crew are all for going to the red light, sleazy section of town known as the Reeperbahn to check out some heavy pornography and catch a sex act or two. I'd done it, seen it, bought the T-shirt in that place when I was 19 so I join up with lighting man Richard Gallup, Henry, Andy, Paul and Seamus to go see The Sugarcubes instead.

The Sugarcubes are okay, not as brilliant as the press has tried to make out, but certainly better than your average Icelandic pop group. We go backstage to say hello and they seem pleased that the Iggy Pop band has come to the show but somewhat disappointed that Iggy himself isn't present. I explain that Mr Pop has to go through an exhaustive session of electroshock therapy after each gig, and they invite us back to their hotel for an Icelandic knees-up.

Much vodka is drunk, and lead singer Björk and I get into an intense rap about punk rock, lava lamps and the necessity for comfortable but sturdy footwear on a long tour, with Andy all the while whispering, "Go on, try and fuck her," in my ear. Well, suffice to say that I don't, and in the early morning Hamburg hours, we wish them well and take our leave.

Monday 14 November – Hamburg, Germany
Awoke at 2pm feeling damn awful after the vodka frenzy of last night. God, that Björk could put the stuff away. For every drink I had, she matched me with two and must have downed at least a bottle and a half of the stuff.

Thai-style soup for the band, from the Eat to the Beat girls, soon had us ship shape and in fighting order.

Soundcheck goes smoothly at our venue for the night, the unlikely-named CCH Saal 3, a massive sports hall. Usual routine of eat, soundcheck, back to hotel, nap, shower and back to venue for the real thing.

Iggy's thigh strain is playing him up again and there's a constant look of pain on his face during the last third of the show. Sound is a bit thin on stage, not nearly as meaty and loud as the soundcheck but sometimes that's how it goes.

Crowd seem pleased though, and two encores are called for.

Backstage, Iggy gives us one of his, "Was I weird? Did I look stupid out there? Am I crazy?" trips which had been so prevalent during the North American tour. At that time we would dispel his paranoia with supportive words and backslaps. At this stage of the game, no-one can be bothered and even Seamus lets out a, "For fuck's sake, shut up!" when Iggy overplays his hand.

Oh yes, boys and girls, life is starting to run fast and mean again.

Tuesday 15 November – Frankfurt, Germany

Luftwaffe... sorry, Lufthansa Flight into sausage town for another show in yet another sports centre. Are they all sports mad here in Germany, or something? Generic, spotless, concrete and glass Stadhalle... very Prussian.

Hotel is nice though. Outside the city centre, surrounded by forests and streams. A great location to smoke a big fat joint, get naked (in the summer months) and run around shouting, "Freedom through Joy!" at the rats, wolves and other wild life.

Evening show is decent enough. Bit ragged in places, with Iggy visiting the audience more than usual, but a fine show nonetheless. Paul disagrees. A self-indulgent outburst from Garristo backstage followed by a predictable couple of hours of bullshit attitude. We ignore him, and I join Andy in Iggy's room back at the hotel to play around with the guitars and work on songs.

Iggy's got a new song which he tentatively titles 'It's On My Body'. He's only recently taught himself to play the guitar so it takes a while to work out what's going on but after a bit, his note-playing hand (his right, Iggy's left-handed) gets quicker, and Andy and I can tell it's a cool song in the making.

Decide we will try it out with the band next soundcheck.

Wednesday 16 November – Düsseldorf, Germany

Very boring day off. Show Iggy the passage in P.J. O'Rourke's new book, *Holidays in Hell*, where it says Iggy moved to Berlin because New York wasn't decadent enough for him. Iggy's observation is, "How would that little ass-wipe know?"

Thursday 17 November – Düsseldorf, Germany

"I was born in Düsseldorf and that is why they call me Rolf..." 'Springtime for Hitler and Germany'. I can't get that goddamn song out of my mind.

Anyway, yes... It is another sports hall, filled to the brim with 4,000 Düsseldorfians – and they love it. Solid, strong playing with even Paul Garristo enjoying himself and Iggy at his spinning, dancing and gyrating finest.

Lord have mercy, there are some fine fräuleins backstage after the show tonight. Some big-chested, peachy-skinned brunette with 'I-wanna-fuck-your-brains-out' eyes, comes on strong. I was hauled away by Henry as Iggy and the band were getting very leery waiting for me in the limo to depart for the hotel.

Jealous bastards.

Later on Jos tells me this particular Prussian sex kitten put on a fine performance for the crew utilising in a very creative way some root vegetables from the dressing room salad. And what do we get to watch back at the hotel...? Sodding CNN, that's what!

Friday 18 November – Munich, Germany

The Bavarians are a special breed of German, very excitable people with a taste for beer and a flair for the dramatic. Good Iggy Pop country.

Our venue for the night is called Circus Krone and it's just that... a bloody circus. Complete with sawdust ring, savage wild animals in cages backstage and the occasional clown.

It's a soundcheck nightmare. My amp blows up after half of 'Kill City' and Iggy says, "Fuck it. Trust in God." Leads us to another fine meal from the Eat to the Beat girls.

Catch a nap at the Munich Hilton before show-time. Will my amp be functioning? Will Andy be eaten by one of the enraged tigers he tries to share his hash stash with? Will Iggy be affected by these surroundings and attempt his own version of the high-wire act and fall...? No, no and no again. Tough and steady. Full-on affirmation and celebration of the here and now with the wild beasts roaring in the background and Iggy as king of this particular jungle.

Sunday 20 November – Zurich, Switzerland

Land in a very cold and snow-laden Zurich. For some reason, today everyone in the band has decided to wear a long black overcoat, and as we get in the limos we look like a bunch of wasted Mafia hitmen on their way to take out some rival mobster.

No soundcheck today as the snow is thick and heavy and Henry and the crew reckon we will do better to wait until the snow ploughs have done their work before attempting to get up to tonight's venue (it's on a steep hill).

Phone my dad and mum in London from the Sheraton Hotel to tell them that I'll be flying over to England after our UK tour to spend Christmas with them. Christmas break... Fuck, yeah! Can't wait.

It's been a solid four and a half months of touring and we are all getting a bit road-sick. Iggy's hurting, Seamus and Paul are tired and grumpy, Andy's on everything but roller-skates and I'm not so slowly turning into a savage drunkard. It's known in the jungle as 'turning native'.

Monday 21 November – Milan, Italy

Looking back on yesterday's entry, I guess I forgot to report on the show. It was a good one. Sold out venue and well worth braving the elements though the ride back to the Sheraton is a little hairy. Deep snow to the left and right of the road with the limo continuously slipping and sliding on a treacherous, ice-ridden surface.

Lay a fair amount of my open bottle of Courvoisier on the lap of Suchi taking a left turn, and as we suddenly swing right to compensate, manage to share some with Iggy's hair. Drive at 15 miles an hour all the way back and are glad of it. This morning, conditions have got worse. After my room service breakfast, I pull open my hotel room curtains to survey a totally white landscape and continuing heavy snowfall. Henry stops by to say it's touch and go whether we will get a flight out today but he reckons it's worth a shot.

Into the limos and another crazy, ice-spinning 15 mile an hour ride to the airport only to find that all flights are cancelled with service not likely to be resumed until tomorrow.

We are due to play a show in Milan tonight. Decision time. The crew and equipment are already in Milan having caught a flight out

last night when the airport was still open. By now, the limos have departed and Iggy, Suchi, Henry and the band complete with luggage have the option of either saying, "Forget it," and catching cabs back to the Sheraton or catching a subway train to Zurich's main railway station to see what's cooking there.

Henry offers up the decision to stay or go to us. Seamus, Paul and Iggy are undecided, but Andy is suddenly transformed into an agent for the spirit of old-time showbiz. "The show must go on... People have paid their money... We don't pull gigs unless we're at death's door." Etc, etc. Every last cliché in the showbiz catalogue. If Andy is an advocate for the defence, I decide it's my moral duty to be the voice of the prosecution. "What? Drag these suitcases through the snow...? Suppose the trains aren't running...? Do you want the whole band to get pneumonia, you maniac...?" Etc, etc. Iggy acknowledges both sides of the argument and comes up with the compromise that we try the train station and if there's nothing moving out to Milan immediately, then we will head back to the hotel and cancel the show.

Well, it turns out there is a train ready to set out for Italy on snow-covered platform one. No porters to help us with the luggage, so a mad dash to the train, after Henry purchases our tickets, dragging our suitcases behind us.

The compartments are spotlessly clean and warm, and as Henry has got us first class seats, you can stretch out and reach a full horizontal position as the Swiss scenery flies by. And what scenery it is. Christmas card images. Small towns covered in thick, white blankets of snow with grey smoke billowing from red brick chimneys. Giant pine trees heavy from the fall. Frozen lakes covered in thick, thick ice that you can drive a heavy truck over without fear of crashing through.

As we continue our journey into the Alps, the car steward serves us dinner. Well, I have to admit that despite my initial reservations, this was turning into quite a ride and I am glad to have caught these views and seen the beauty of the Swiss Alps in these conditions.

After four hours, I notice there is a lot less snow about with portions of green fields visible and trees free of white branches. A half hour later, the snow has vanished completely and we are pulling into Milano station.

Our promoter, Franco Manone, is waiting with a couple of cabs and we drive quickly through the streets of Milan to our venue, The Rolling Stone Club, having just enough time to take off our coats before stepping onto the stage.

At that point my diary entries got decidedly deranged. The November 22nd to 27th instalments are pretty much unintelligible, which I put down to a spate of heavy recreational drinking with Andy, combined with a savage dose of tour fatigue.

For instance, here's my diary entry for 25 November, minus the blood and brandy stains.

Friday 25 November – Madrid, Spain
BASTARDS! BASTARDS!… Vicious swine, I'll show you. Fucking with me indeed… Fuck, fuck, bollocks and good night.

Frightening, isn't it? I haven't got a clue who the vicious swine were or what I needed to show them.

Anyway, by the 28th I'd pulled myself together enough to resume my usual diary service.

Monday 28 November – Bordeaux, France
A five hour drive with Iggy and Suchi in a silver Merc from San Sebastian, Spain across the French border into the home of the finest wines in the world, Bordeaux.

Nice town. Iggy digs the architecture and agrees with me that Jos is way off base in his belief that the French are a weak and spineless people. We're both of the opinion that they know what's what and that the French women are most fine and très chic

The venue is a very pompous-sounding Salles des Fêtes de Grands Parcs, an ugly metal-walled modern building that looks more like a garage than a music club. No soundcheck as everyone is ill again, so

IGGY POP + CRAZYHEAD

24 NOVIEMBRE BARCELONA 25 NOVIEMBRE MADRID 27 NOVIEMBRE - SAN SEBASTIAN

downed some of our English cooks' hot chicken noodle soup for some energy. After a nap at the hotel, back to the Salle des Fêtes etc, etc, for a low-action, auto-pilot type of show. Don't even take a glass of wine back at the hotel, as we all feel too flu-ish. Everyone just makes for their rooms and locks their doors.

Still, just Paris to go and then we will be in England with a short UK tour to complete before we finally get some time off for Christmas. There's light at the end of the tunnel, and it's getting brighter.

Wednesday 30 November – Paris, France

The last of two shows here in the city of lights. Yesterday's performance was a real gas. A firing on all cylinders Parisian spectacle. Iggy is a god here. The French really love their rock 'n' roll, and both shows at our compact 1,500 seat theatre/venue, La Cigale, had sold out weeks ago.

Tonight, we are more than prepared for another hot and sweaty performance. Through the firmly-established pre-gig traditions of nap, shower etc, with the newly added addition of raiding the hotel room mini-bar of its chocolates for some artificial energy for the show.

Each of the band seems to have a different way of achieving the same results. Iggy's is swallowing half a jar of honey, washed down with strong black coffee. Paul's is fruit, whilst Seamus gets off on sweet tea and a cigarette. Andy's source of energy... Well, need I bother to record that?

This gig is a monster – emotional and transcendental – a rock 'n' roll triumph. champagne and the crème de la crème of Parisian demi-monde backstage, along with old faces like ex-Dead Boys and Lords of the New Church singer, Stiv Bators. Small talk, joints, more champagne and an invitation from our French A&M Records representative, Claire, to eat some dinner at the La Palace nightclub. French cooking, fine wines and cool conversation. At the restaurant, people recognising us from the show, step over to slap our backs and thank us for 'ze great rock and roll'.

Last show of our continental European tour. Tomorrow, we fly British Airways to Heathrow Airport, London, to begin a 15 date tour of Great Britain, followed by a much needed two week vacation. Two weeks off the rock 'n' roll roller-coaster. Fourteen days in London to do as I please. When I like. With no particular place to go. Almost...

Free at last, free at last, free at last...

NIGHT AND DAY

Iggy walked into the room wearing the dark blue uniform of an Air Force colonel. I knew his rank, and that it was an Air Force uniform, because above a chestful of campaign medals there were large silver wings and A.F. COLONEL OSTERBERG in gold, embroidered letters. He had matching jodhpurs on, tucked into knee high leather riding boots, and in his left hand he carried a riding crop which he tapped against his boots as he swaggered by. I remember thinking, what the Hell does an Air Force colonel want with riding boots? But after a couple of seconds it started to make a twisted kind of sense.

Iggy wasn't the only man in uniform. Alongside me, sitting at a wooden table were the other members of the band, each in some form of military dress. Andy had on a red tunic with gold epaulettes and a fetching kilt. Although the man didn't really look much like Andy facially, I knew it had to be him because he sported cowboy boots and a big felt hat, and was constantly chain smoking and drooling on himself. Beside him sat Seamus in dark glasses wearing an olive green jump-suit complete with olive green tin helmet. Paul was in camouflage battle fatigues and a black beret, and I felt slightly annoyed at the fact that I was in exactly the same fatigues/beret combination as him.

Iggy passed us and climbed onto a small wooden platform where he danced and preened while whistling Cole Porter's 'Night and Day'. There was a kind of strobe effect going on in the room; a set of faulty fluorescent ceiling lights were flickering at different speeds making Iggy's dance look fractured and fragmented. Slow, then fast… slow… then very fast again.

There were no windows in the room; I hadn't a clue where we were but, instinctively knew we had to be below ground. Maybe a concrete bunker or an air raid shelter. Iggy bought his dancing to an end with a mighty crack of his riding crop against the side of his right boot. He came to attention and addressed us.

"Okay, you rock 'n' roll fuckers, listen up!" Iggy raised a hand above his head and pulled down a large map of the world. He pointed his riding crop at the United States.

"There. Remember? A generally successful mission with light casualties. McCoy took a flesh wound and I was under some heavy flak in Miami, but we got on with the job and honour was satisfied."

As Iggy turned and faced us from the map, I noticed he had instantly grown a thin moustache. There seemed nothing unusual about this at the time.

Iggy moved his crop south and continued. "Brazil, Argentina... A complete success. Local resistance annihilated and a strong outpost established for future campaigns. Any questions?"

As the four of us shook our heads from side to side in unison, I noticed that Paul and Seamus had swapped uniforms. Again, there seemed nothing unusual about this at the time.

Iggy shouted, "Good," did a quick soft-shoe shuffle, spun around in a full circle, clicked his boot heels together and pointed to another part of the map. "The European invasion, gentlemen. We fought the motherfuckers on the beaches, we fought them in the clubs and theatres, and we came out smiling. Gibbs."

I stood up. "Yes."

"Gibbs, we seemed to lose contact with you at one point during the big push. What have you to say?"

"Well, during the Benelux assault, I was the victim of a fifth columnist... The enemy within."

I looked over at Andy but his face was hidden by clouds of dense smoke from sucking on a joint that must have been all of two foot long. Iggy was sympathetic.

"Not to worry. Don't let it happen again, and let's hear no more about it."

I sat back down. "No, sir. Thank you, Jim."

Iggy pointed out other European countries. "Scandinavia... A direct hit. Germany... A hard pounding but the Hun know a good thing when they hear it. Spain... Well, fuck, you can't win 'em all. France... Complete capitulation. Victory, victory, utter victory." Iggy moved his crop across the Channel. "The United Kingdom followed and I realised this would be our biggest test."

Paul stood up. "I'd just like to say at this point, that you should fuck that shit..."

Iggy ignored him. "Tough nut to crack, the UK. Morale was low. I knew that all too well. We were looking directly into the pitiful pus-filled face of defeat, gentlemen. A long campaign reaching its climax with ammunition spent..." Iggy placed his head in his hands and sobbed, "The horror, the horror."

Paul was still on his feet. "I would just like to say at this point that Elvis was a vicious, white-trash lesbian."

Iggy continued to ignore him. "But despite the odds, you pulled it off, brave boys. Tough rock 'n' roll fuckers. You're worth a million in prizes."

At that point, the map of the world shot upwards and a massive Stars and Stripes slowly lowered like a piece of scenery, behind Iggy. Confetti fell from the ceiling and Seamus played 'The Times They Are A-Changing' on a fur-covered mouth organ.

Iggy stepped off the platform and stood before us. "Enjoy your leave, men. You've earned it."

With that, Iggy saluted and marched past us and out of a door at the back of the room. Andy, Paul and Seamus followed him out, but I continued to sit. The Stars and Stripes had become an electric flag, flashing red, white and blue, giving off that eerie, pulsating hum that neon signs produce when it rains.

Then the room turned black. What the Hell...? I couldn't see my hand in front of my face. I stumbled around in the darkness, desperately feeling for the door, knowing it was somewhere close but only discovering the sensation of my fingertips on smooth painted walls.

It was a surreal and crazy dream, and when I woke from it, I found myself still surrounded by the darkness. It was one of those feverish, fearful moments when on awaking, you're not sure of where, who or how. Was I in New York? Paris? Tel Aviv? As my eyes grew accustomed to the dark, I saw a bedside lamp and switched it on. There lying beside me was my wife, and things started to come into focus. Realisation. Yeah, London... Christmas Eve... two weeks of rest and recuperation after the final climactic show of the UK Tour five days past.

I quietly slid out of bed and went to the kitchen to pour myself a drink. I considered that dream and put it down to too many chemicals and the war movie I had watched on the TV earlier, with George C. Scott as General Patton. My hands were shaking and I felt restless and anxious.

I'd been looking forward to the break in touring for weeks, but when it had finally arrived, I found myself in the grip of severe rock 'n' roll withdrawal symptoms.

Iggy had flown to Thailand for the holidays, with Suchi. Paul was in New York, and Andy back in Los Angeles. Seamus was somewhere in London, as I was, having rented a flat in West Hampstead at the northern end of the city. This was my base during the Christmas break through into the New Year, with visits and gift-giving and big festive dinners at parents, sisters and friends about town. But that Christmas Eve, with 12 days of our vacation still to go, I was already seriously missing the touring lifestyle. The free time and lack of musical activity that went with it was bearing down heavily on my psyche.

This was not unusual for me. I had suffered this kind of post-tour cold turkey many times before. When you go from having a purpose to your day, of having a destination, having the glamour and excitement of travelling from city to city, hotel to hotel, of performing nightly for large numbers of excited, enthusiastic people. When you go from that to the mundane slow-moving everyday world, it can prove a big downer. Climbing off a world tour of that intensity is like trying to step out of a car doing 90 miles an hour in the impossible hope that you can come to a dead stop when your feet meet the tarmac. Some kind of injury will be sustained.

I took the litre bottle of vodka from the kitchen and sat and drank and sat and drank some more 'til the anxiety evaporated and sleep engulfed me. It seemed the only way to handle it. My wife found me sprawled out on the fireside rug on Christmas morning still clutching the empty bottle to my chest. She shook me awake.

"Happy Christmas," I said. Noticing the empty booze container, I added, "we wouldn't happen to have any more vodka about, would we?"

There seemed nothing unusual about this at the time.

BLOWFISH

Despite my initial reaction to the holiday, I did come to relax and enjoy the second half of our 14 day respite. I enjoyed having the time and the money to take out my wife, family and friends to fancy London restaurants without regard to the cost. I enjoyed seeing in the New Year with expensive champagne and familiar faces, and telling tales of my touring adventures. Still, it did come as a relief on the fifth day of 1989 to pack my suitcase once more, leave London and rejoin the Iggy Pop bandwagon.

A two week revisit of Europe followed. Gigs in Holland, Belgium, France and Italy, during which time we celebrated the birthdays of Seamus and Suchi with cake and champagne, and sampled the ample delights of cities such as Nice, Paris (again), Florence and Naples.

On Friday 20 January, we hitched a 14 hour ride out of Rome on a JAL wide-bodied jet to the island of Honshu, setting down in the capital of Japan, Tokyo.

Now Japan and all things Japanese had held a fascination for me since I was a young boy. I had loved the Samurai movies of Akira Kurosawa, and the ronin with no name, played by Toshiro Mifune. I had studied the Japanese martial arts of Aikido and Shorinji Kempo, and admired the wood-block prints of such artists as Hokusai and Hiroshige. And so it was with a real sense of anticipation that I disembarked from our plane at Narita Airport and lined up with the band to go through customs.

Andy was the first up to open his suitcases for inspection and play Mister Clean. This was not a natural role for Andy. He had come back from his Christmas break in LA with two nasty-looking black eyes which his then wife had given him for some misdemeanour or other. Over the two weeks, those swollen eyes had turned from their original blue-black colour to a putrid green-yellow hue. This, combined with his usual dishevelled Scandinavian hippy attire, had given Andy the appearance of a man who had foregone sleep for several days in favour of some drug-related bad craziness.

Going through customs with Andy McCoy is a lottery at the best of times. Going through Japanese customs with him, with their ultra-heavy attitude towards drugs and severe penalties for possession, gave a whole new dimension of apprehension to this ritual. After all, this was the place where that devoted husband and family man, Paul McCartney, had been busted for possession of marijuana back in 1980. The result was jail, humiliation, deportation, a cancelled tour and a ban from entering Japan for a year. So, with McCoy, that chemically driven playboy of the Western world, before me having his clothes checked by a thorough and serious-looking customs official, I couldn't help thinking that we could be only seconds away from the termination of our Japanese tour.

It was with some relief that I saw the customs official, seemingly satisfied, slam shut Andy's suitcase and wave him through. Thank Christ for that, I thought. Then it was my turn to deal with that stone-faced, cold fish of a man.

"What's this?" he asked. He had pulled out a copy of the soft-porn magazine *Mayfair* from my suitcase and was holding it up to my face.

"Oh, that," I replied. "Yes... Well, that's a magazine for men rather like *Playboy* or *Penthouse.*"

He flicked through it and announced in a cold disapproving voice, "It is not allowed."

"Really? But I've been to your country before and seen similar magazines on sale with naked women in them."

This was an argument he was fully prepared for. Opening up the magazine again, he pointed directly to some woman's pussy in the 'Readers' Wives' section – regular readers of these magazines will know exactly what I mean – and said, "But they don't show this."

I was amazed. "What? They show naked women but not their snatches?"

"Yes," he snapped.

"How about men's cocks...? You know, when there's photos of couples doing it, is it also illegal to show a man's penis?"

His voice was adamant. "Yes. We do not allow such things."

It was all very interesting. Just minutes into my return to this country, I had received a new and valuable insight into the Japanese mind.

I surrendered my copy of *Mayfair.*

On entering my hotel room at the Tokyo Hilton some hours later, I discovered this boycott of genitalia was an epidemic. Among the various cable channels on my TV was a porno station which boasted 24 hours of fucking and sucking. Thing was, whenever any of the 'f and s' took place, where the chick's pussy or the man's dick should have been, that portion of the TV screen would suddenly be engulfed by a bizarre electronic effect that would totally cover up the action. Tits – fine. Asses – sure. Genitals – forget it, pal...! What are you, a pervert or something?

That night, our promoter, Massy Hayashi, splashed out on a welcoming traditional-style Japanese dinner for us at a Tokyo restaurant with paper screen walls and low tables. Hot sake was served by kimono-clad waitresses

and after picking with chopsticks at the variety of dishes set before us, we were asked what we would like for a main course.

Iggy announced he was in the mood for a fresh tuna sashimi to give him plenty of energy for the shows to come. It was fresh alright. A large plate was placed before him containing slices of thinly cut tuna delicately displayed around the edge of the dish. Slap in the middle of the plate, still flapping around and rapidly opening and closing its mouth in its death throes, was the fish that the meat had just been cut from. It had been impaled on a bamboo skewer and placed there as some kind of grotesque, macabre decoration, its body devoid of any flesh from its tail to its head with its white central bones clearly visible.

Now I'm no Saint Francis of Assisi you understand, having fished and boiled live lobster and eaten the flesh of animals all my life, but even for me, this was too much. My instinct was to grab that hapless fish off the plate and put it out of its misery with a swift blow. But this was Japan, this was their way, their culture, and if I had done that, it would have been a direct insult to our host, Mr Hayashi.

Instead, I looked away until Suchi informed me that the poor tuna had finally given up the ghost.

"Shit," I said to no-one in particular, "I thought these people were Buddhists."

I didn't feel much like eating after that but Iggy, totally unphased by the cruel demise of the fish, tucked into his fresh, fresh tuna slices with relish. After a while, my appetite returned and I ordered tempura, a dish of vegetables and pre-killed prawns and shrimp, deep fried in batter. This particular dish was passed on by the Portuguese sailors who traded with Japan in the 17th century; as with all things from the outside that the Japanese had been exposed to, they had refined it and made it their own.

This is the great historical trait of the Japanese nation. Japan is an oyster that absorbs the grains of influence washed up by the West and turns them into its own unique pearls.

That following day, the jet lag kicked in bad. As a couple of taxis made their way through the rush hour Tokyo traffic carrying the band to soundcheck, I kept slipping in and out of consciousness, unable to resist the waves of drowsiness that washed over me.

Iggy was already in the dressing room on our arrival, having spent a couple of hours at our Sun Plaza venue giving interviews and pressing the flesh with the press. He could see I was more ready for bed than soundcheck, and poured me a cup of coffee so strong it could have floated an iron witch.

"I know how you feel," he said. "Been drinking this coffee all day just to stay awake myself. Hang on in there. It will pass."

Two or three more cups of that pitch black Java later, I started to feel like a functioning human being again.

The Sun Plaza was a 2,000 all-seater modern theatre situated in a shopping mall type complex in the Shinjuku district of Tokyo. Ultra clean, staid and completely devoid of any kind of atmosphere.

As we took to the stage at 6.30pm precisely, to polite applause, I felt more like a teacher about to take school assembly for a bunch of sixth formers, than a member of a rock 'n' roll band.

'Til about the middle of the set, the audience just sat there releasing the identical amounts of polite applause after each song. Their manner suggested a bunch of curious anthropologists closely studying a newly-discovered tribe of savage ape men. Then, two things happened that changed the situation completely.

First, Iggy decided enough was enough and swallow-dived off the stage onto the front row of seated Japanese, who just managed to register various expressions of horror before he landed on top of them. I guess they weren't used to that kind of thing and their reflexes were pretty dull. Iggy all but flattened several of the poor fools who hadn't realised that you're supposed to catch an incoming Iggy missile. This sent the Sun Plaza uniformed security men into a mouth-foaming frenzy. Dozens of them descended on the landing spot, grabbing wildly at Iggy's legs vertically sticking up in the air, his upper torso having disappeared behind the front seats with his head wedged in some terminally-embarrassed chick's crotch.

I laughed so much I was nearly sick, and when I turned and looked at Paul, he had a fit of hysterics so bad that he had dropped one of his sticks and was in danger of falling off his drum stool.

Then Andy made his move.

Despite not having brought along Iggy's dancing surface, we were told that we still could not smoke on stage as the Japanese have extremely tough fire regulations concerning public places. In the confusion caused by Iggy's frighteningly authentic impersonation of a V2 rocket, Andy probably thought nobody would notice if he sneaked in a quick couple of drags of a ciggie. He was wrong. No sooner had the fag been lit than more perplexed looking security men rushed onto the stage from the wings, surrounding Andy with fire extinguishers and hysterically shouting, "Iie, iie... Abunai, abunai!" (No, no... It's dangerous, it's dangerous!)

What a scene! Iggy still unintentionally investigating that poor girl's groin in the second row, his legs waving around like a couple of windswept banners. On stage, Andy about to be stomped on by the nicotine police, moving in for the kill with their buckets of sand and foam extinguishers.

It was Kafka meets the Keystone Cops. But the effect of all this was that the previously stiffly sitting, conformist audience had risen to their feet. Some had even dared to rush down to the front of the stage to catch all the action.

Once Andy had surrendered his cigarette and Iggy had made it back to the stage, the gig took on a whole different shape. More and more members of an increasingly rebellious audience left their seats and ran down to the stage-front to dance and get crazy. At the Sun Plaza, this was the equivalent of doing a streak through the House of Lords whilst screaming, 'You're all a

bunch of useless old bastards,' through a megaphone. Well, maybe not quite... But you get the picture. The security men did their best to stop the rebels but, in the end they were overwhelmed by the sheer numbers and realising that it was as hopeless as trying to catch a waterfall in a paper cup, they gave up. From then on, it became a rock 'n' roll show.

After the gig, the band and crew had dinner at a Korean Barbecue restaurant where each table had a gas-fired habachi on which to cook your favourite items from a selection of pork, beef, vegetables and seafood.

Iggy and Suchi hadn't joined us. They had an invitation from the famous Japanese composer and musician, Ryuichi Sakamoto, for dinner across town. It was quite a surprise when both turned up at the Korean looking none too pleased, just as we were getting into our third round of beers and sake.

"What happened?" I asked.

Iggy could hardly contain his anger. "It was fuckin' embarrassing. Sakamoto pulled up in his limo just as we arrived at the restaurant. He got out, said he had something else on and that we'd get together another time. Then he drove off in the limo leaving Suchi and me just standing there in the fuckin' rain."

Even normally placid Suchi was bugged. "I can't believe he did that to Jim. It was so rude."

This sorry tale produced fighting talk from all listeners. Jos was all for getting a lynch mob together to track down Sakamoto and teach him a lesson. Seamus kept repeating, "What a cunt. What an utter cunt."

With each successive beer, the revenge plans hardened up 'til a bunch of us were seriously baying for blood.

Iggy decided to calm things down. "I'm thankful for your loyalty but kicking Sakamoto's ass won't help."

We let off steam back at the Hilton by taking to pieces Andy's hotel room instead. McCoy led the way.

"Fuck that asshole." ...SMASH... Andy put his cowboy boot through the 28 inch Sony TV set. "Yeah, fuck him!"...CRASH... My well-aimed bottle of Kirin beer shattered the wall mirror. ...RIP... Paul yanked out the telephone and chucked it out of the open hotel window where it fell seven floors to bounce across the road below.

The next morning, after changing Yankee dollars for yen, we all chipped in to pay for the damage. Everyone agreed it was worth every penny.

*

Following a limo ride to Tokyo's second airport, Haneda, we boarded a jet bound for Osaka. As the plane gained in altitude, I looked down and caught a glimpse of snow-capped Mount Fuji below us. A potent symbol of Japan. A beautiful jewel.

On arriving at our Osaka Hotel, the Grand, we were greeted by crowds of adoring Japanese girl fans, most of whom were there to give presents to, and have their photos taken with, Andy. His old band, Hanoi Rocks, had been huge in Japan. With their glam, pretty boy looks and catchy non-threatening power pop songs, Hanoi had been embraced by the Japanese youth as the perfect Western rock group. In Japan, it was obvious that Andy had a bigger profile than Iggy, and at first, McCoy basked in the attention and fame. When we had first arrived, he received the various small gifts from his fans with grace and gratitude.

"Oh thank you, darlin'... How wonderful... I'm so lucky to have a fan like you." By Osaka, though, this unnatural behaviour on Andy's part could no longer be sustained. "Fuck... Not another pair of chopsticks. Can't you give me something useful... like hash?"

Andy had a solo album out in Japan, and his Japanese record company had sent a representative to Osaka to buy him drinks and dinner, and basically look after his every whim. This rep became known as the Midnight Emperor, because Andy would generally call his room at that hour with demands for booze, drugs and anything else that took his fancy. I can't remember how the Emperor part got added, but I guess Andy's Imperial behaviour somehow got mixed up with the record rep's title, as he really should have been referred to as the Midnight Slave.

Now, Andy can just about run bull shit rings around anyone, and this poor sod had no defence against the McCoy ego, being one of life's natural-born innocents. He became Andy's obedient servant; but it wasn't until the end of our Japanese visit that I discovered just how sucked into McCoy's bad craziness he had been.

On the day of our Osaka show, I decided I had to go see Osaka Castle, as so far, my Japanese experience had consisted of a daily diet of hotel, soundcheck, hotel, gig, restaurant, bar and hotel. Julie, our interpreter, ordered up a taxi and joined Seamus and I for the ride. No-one else in the band seemed interested.

The cab took us up to the moat gate of the castle, which we walked through to get to the main building. It was a spectacular sight. An eight level

Samurai fortress, copper green and ivory, towering above us. A magnificent reminder of Japan's Bushido legacy.

As we made our way from floor to floor, we viewed the collection of katana (Samurai swords), armour and historical artefacts, and I discovered the story of Osaka Castle.

Completed in 1586, the fortress had taken two and a half years to build. It employed 60,000 labourers, and a huge volume of stones were carried to Osaka on more than 1,000 vessels from various parts of the country. It was the seat of power for the then shogun (military dictator) Toyotomi Hideyoshi who had conquered, unified and ruled Japan from 1589 'til his death in 1598.

As well as being a successful warrior, Hideyoshi was also a lover of poetry, music and the arts. He was a patron of a flamboyant, artistic style known as Momoyama, notable for its lavish use of gold lacquer and vivid rich colours. There were many fine examples of Momoyama screens, scrolls and paintings in Osaka Castle; just being able to lose myself in their viewing left me feeling replenished and renewed.

You know, touring musicians can sometimes forget what an enviable situation they are in. Travelling the world from city to city, we tend to sacrifice opportunities for exposure to another country's history and culture at the altar of laziness and ignorance. The amount of musicians I have asked on their return from a visit to Rome or Athens or Kyoto, "Well, what did you do there?" only to receive as a reply the old hedonistic mantra of, "Well, we played some rock 'n' roll, got wasted and got laid," is depressingly high.

Of course, sometimes you don't have the time, or are genuinely exhausted from a heavy schedule. But for me, being a musician has proved to be my university and my education. It has schooled me in the ways of other cultures, and shaped my view of the world and its people. It is important to keep learning and use any available time as well as possible.

I was physically tired, with no time for rest before that evening's Osaka show, but I still felt the trip to Hideyoshi's fortress had been well worth the effort.

The Osaka gig was a whole different can of sushi from the Tokyo show. It was pandemonium from song one, with a kamikaze crowd launching themselves over and through the stage-front barriers to dive back into the arms of the audience just before worried-looking security guards could reach them.

Back at the Osaka Grand, a large contingent of giggling excited girls awaited our arrival in the lobby.

Japanese groupies are really organised. They have a communication and spy network that would make MI5 and the CIA blush with envy. They have a fanatical devotion to their objectives. Long before a favourite band or artist even gets to Japan, these girls will have discovered appointment times and locations, hotels and room numbers, and even the restaurants where their targets will be wined and dined by respective record companies. They will have scoured the Japanese music magazines for interviews and information for gift ideas, and to discover the likes, dislikes and interests of those they intend to get to know in the biblical sense. Their research is thorough.

I also noticed that most of them were not exactly short of money. The same faces turned up at show after show all over the country, usually staying at the same hotels as the band. Added to the concert ticket prices and travel expenses, this must have required a small fortune to be invested in a venture that didn't exactly guarantee a return.

There was a pair of real pretty girls who sheepishly walked up to me when I ordered myself a drink at the Osaka Grand's cocktail bar. Porcelain-skinned dolls, both taller than the average Japanese woman, with a touch of catwalk strut to their movements. One of them gave me a heart-melting smile and handed me a beautifully wrapped package.

"What's this?" I asked.

"A gift... I hope you like," she answered. It was so exquisitely bound that it seemed a pity to open it up. When I did, I found a richly coloured book containing various wood-block prints of Mount Fuji by my favourite Japanese artist, Hokusai. Beside each print, on the adjoining page, was an appropriate five line haiku poem, written in both English and Kanji (Chinese characters).

"It's wonderful," I told her. "But how did you know that I was a big fan of Hokusai's?"

"I just know," she said.

This seemed like a suitable time to put to use my slender knowledge of the Japanese language. "Domo arrigato gozaimashita?" I told her. (Thank you for what you have done.)

"Do itashimashite," she replied. (It was nothing.)

I pointed to a couple of bar stools beside me and asked them what they would like to drink. Strangely enough, they requested vodka-tonics, which was what I was drinking. Their names were Noriko and Kumi, and they were both from Yokohama. I asked them what they thought about a fellow Japanese woman, Suchi, marrying the wild man of rock, Iggy Pop.

"Oh, Suchi is very famous for Japanese girl music fans," Noriko said.

"Really? Is Suchi a kind of role model for you all?"

"Yes," Kumi nodded enthusiastically. "We all wish to do as Suchi has done. She became wife of her hero."

This was all very interesting. Later, it got me thinking about the relationship between Iggy and Suchi. Obviously, Suchi had a major role to play in the maintenance of the new career-orientated, chemically reformed and (offstage) moderate Iggy Pop. By his own admission, Iggy had a quick temper, and we had seen many examples of this, combined with his impatient nature, during the tour. But on nearly all occasions, Suchi was able to get through to him and stop the situations escalating by pleading for calm and pointing out his irrationality. Iggy, in turn, valued his wife's ability to change his reckless behaviour. As well as pouring cold water on his sometimes hot-headed conduct, Suchi also seemed to be an important and trusted source of advice for Iggy. She generally offered an opinion on his clothing decisions for stage and video shoots, and gave counsel on his performances and stage presentation. Whether Suchi had much involvement in Iggy's business decisions and career moves. I don't know. But she was, without doubt, an influence and a substantial source of much needed stability in Iggy's life.

From Osaka we flew an hour south to the city of Fukuoka. Japan is made up of four islands, Hokkaido in the north, the central and largest island of Honshu where the capital, Tokyo, resides. Shikoku in the south east with Fukuoka sitting on the north west coast of the southern-most island of Kyushu.

The night of our descent into Fukuoka, we discovered that the wild Osaka crowd was an aberration from the general norm of polite applause and contained excitement exhibited by audiences in the rest of the country. It was a very lukewarm kind of show in Fukuoka, for a very lukewarm kind of crowd.

As this was our last gig in Japan, our agency, H.I.P., really pulled out all the stops for our after-show dinner. An entire traditional-style Japanese restaurant was hired for the exclusive use of the band and crew. Dozens of earthenware bottles of hot sake, ice cold Japanese beer, sashimi, sushi and dish after dish of local delicacies were delivered to our tables by traditionally dressed Fukuoka girls who looked like they had just stepped out of an 18th century Ukiyoe painting.

I had noticed a wooden fish sign suspended over the restaurant door when we arrived, and understood its meaning: the establishment had a chef who was qualified and certified to prepare the particularly tasty, very expensive and potentially dangerous raw flesh of the Pacific blowfish. This particular fish has an extremely deadly poison residing in its liver, and if so much as a tiny amount finds its way onto the blowfish sashimi, the result would probably be death for the eater. Half a dozen or so Japanese diners die this way every year. As a result, it is considered a very special delicacy and costs an astronomical amount. On the other side of the table, the head of H.I.P., Massy Hayashi, was congratulating Iggy on another successful tour. I called out to him, to try to secure a rare opportunity.

"Hey, Massy, I see they serve blowfish sashimi. Would it be possible for me to try some?"

"Sure," he said, "but are you aware of the risks?"

I told him I knew all about it and if I dropped down dead at the table, I would not hold him responsible and come back to haunt him.

"Good," he said, and with a wide smile added, "I would hate to have been haunted by an Iggy Pop bass player. You would have been a very noisy ghost."

Henry had caught wind of what was going on at the end of the table. "Gibbs, I don't want you risking your life over the eating of some damn cold fish... We've still got shows to do, goddammit."

"Relax, Henry," I replied, "I've left all my remaining p.d.s to you in my will, and taught all the necessary bass parts to Joss by direct psychic communication."

Fifteen minutes or so later, my plate of death or glory sashimi was placed before me. As I picked up the first piece and popped it into my mouth, I noticed that all eyes were on me.

"It's delicious, you morbid bastards," I declared, and offered up the blowfish for someone else to try. By their reactions, you would have thought I was offering them radioactively contaminated human flesh. "Here, Seamus, try a slice," I said, passing him the plate.

"No way! You won 't get me to eat that stuff."

"How about you, Paul?" I persisted.

"Fuck that shit!" was Garristo's predictable response. Iggy made some lame excuse along the lines that he thought he had tried it once before and didn't much like it. Even that connoisseur of poisons and arch-poisoner himself, Andy McCoy, declined to risk life and limb by taking a bite.

"What a bunch of pussies," I said, and ate up all the sashimi myself, at one point taking a break from my food to pretend to Henry that I'd suddenly come over queer with intense stomach pains. If I'd persisted with this charade, Henry would have had a coronary, so I let him off the hook by telling him that it was all make believe. I noticed he continued to keep a watchful eye on me for the remainder of the dinner.

Back at the hotel, Noriko, who had travelled on from Osaka, was waiting for me outside my room door with another present. This time it was a bottle of good quality sake.

"Where's Kumi?" I asked.

"She's not come to Fukuoka as I told her I wanted to see you alone."

Oh no! I'd had a skinful of sake at the restaurant with the inevitable result that my libido was up and my resistance was down, and now this high-cheekboned beauty was making her move. These girls really know what they're doing. It became a battle between testosterone and common sense, with testosterone the likely victor. I grabbed her arm and pushed my key into the door with the intention of leading her into my room for a long, uninterrupted night of outrageous sex. But then, the memory of the Stray Cats affair and Henry's previous warnings about statutory rape interceded; I cursed my ability to conjure up such thoughts at a time like this. I settled for a lingering kiss in the corridor, instead.

"Look," I said, "I really like you but I'm tired and drunk and have to get up early to fly to New Zealand tomorrow so..."

She was upset but said she understood, and walked down the corridor and into the elevator. Five minutes later, in my room, I changed my mind. I bolted back down the corridor and took the stairway to the lobby, only to find that she had gone. It was just as well.

The next morning, I woke up fully clothed in bed with the empty sake bottle that Noriko had given me on my bedside table, and the TV still on showing a variety of electronically-castrated porno stars in non-action on the 'f and s' cable channel.

At Narita airport later that day, Andy ordered Midnight Emperor around for the last time, "Hey, get me some beer... I wanna sandwich... Gimme some money. I'll pay you back the next time I get to Japan."

I noticed McCoy's slave was looking pretty awful. His skin was unnaturally pale, he had acquired glazed, bombed-out eyes and seemed shaky. I went and sat next to Andy in the airport restaurant to ask him about this, but first Andy had an observation of his own.

"Alvin, man, you were really fucked up last night."

"Was I? I thought I behaved pretty well at the H.I.P. dinner."

Andy continued, "No, not there. After. Don't you remember? You came into my room about 3am looking for some chick, knocked my TV onto the floor and fell over a chair."

I had no recollection of that whatsoever. "Never mind about all that," I said, not wanting to get side-tracked. "What the Hell has happened to the Midnight Emperor. He looks terrible. Is he ill or something?"

"Oh, that's probably the smack."

"What smack?" I asked. "Midnight never exactly struck me as the user type."

"No, he wasn't," Andy continued. "Until I got him to get some and turned him on."

"What? You got that poor bastard on brown?"

"Yeah," Andy said, "he really likes it now."

Barely hiding my disgust, I coldly asked a rhetorical question, "You must be a proud man, McCoy."

With an utterly serious tone of voice, came Andy's reply. "I am," he said, "I am."

COLA WARS

"Hey, Alvin, you wouldn't happen to be an Englishman, would you? Ha, ha ha! Ha ha ha!" Iggy had just arrived at our dressing room in Wellington, New Zealand, and immediately noticed my glowing, lobster-red, sunburned face and arms.

"Yes, Jim, laugh now," I retaliated, "but when I turn up at your door with my attorney to take you to the cleaners for this debilitating industrial injury, we'll find out if you still see the funny side."

The extreme sunburn was, of course, all my own fault. Our venue, Athletic Park, was a large rugby football stadium a short drive from Wellington City Centre. As the band had hung around in the hot afternoon sun, waiting for the equipment to be set up for the soundcheck, I decided I'd lose the unbecoming pale pallor I'd acquired over the winter months by catching some rays, sprawled out on the grass pitch. I'd only laid out there for 30 minutes or so, but I completely underestimated the depletion of ozone in this part of the world. By the time we'd made it back to our hotel after the 'check, my face was swollen and sore and doing a fine impression of a barbecued piece of meat.

Neither had the soundcheck itself exactly gone to plan. Since Europe, we had had to forego our personal equipment and rely on each promoter to provide the correct stipulated amplifiers, drums etc. Generally, good quality equipment had been provided, but there are always exceptions to the rule. After the clockwork perfection of the Japanese tour, we should have realised that this would be the place for the exception.

Seamus's Fender twin amp sounded ill and fucked. Paul's drum kit was a disgrace, and Andy's Marshalls on close inspection turned out not to be Marshalls at all. The only decent amp on the stage was my authentic Ampeg bass stack. Now, if this had been at an earlier time during the world tour, we would have yelled and snarled, thrown things around backstage and got Henry to physically threaten the promoter. But with just two shows to play in Kiwi, and a two week stint in Australia to go 'til the Iggy Pop bandwagon rolled no more, we handled it instead with shrugs and so-whats, and even laughed at the bizarre farting sounds emanating from Seamus's sad amplifier.

As I plastered some more of Suchi's moisturising cream on my stinging flesh at the dressing room mirror, Henry and production manager Mark Edwards came in to escort us down to the stage. We were second to the headline act on a festival bill titled 'Barnestorming'. It was so titled because the headliner was a Scottish Australian singer by the name of Jimmy Barnes who had once been in a band called Cold Chisel which, according to various New Zealanders and Australians I'd spoken to, had been one of the finest rock bands ever to grace both those countries' shores. Apparently, Chisel had split up in the late 70s and Mr Barnes had gone on to find fame and glory in this part of the world as a solo singer with a variety of backing bands. I'd never heard of either Cold Chisel or Jimmy Barnes, but our NZ promoter assured us, "Jimmy ain't no poofter and he's as big as you can get in the Antipodes."

Quite.

Two local-ish bands had already warmed up the Fosters-supping crowd which, as we approached the stage, looked to be about 20,000 strong. I had high hopes, despite the dodgy equipment, that we would blow J.B. and his musical hacks off the stage with our new streamlined back to basics set. But as we stepped onto the boards to confront the extremely drunk and rowdy mob of an audience, I spotted a couple of stage accessories that I realised might detract Iggy's focus from that aim.

Directly behind the amplifiers and kit hung a massive backdrop declaring: 'PEPSI COLA – THE VOICE OF A NEW GENERATION' in red and blue letters on a white canvas background. Furthermore, flapping around in the early evening breeze on both sides of the stage were two ten foot banners bearing the Pepsi trademark along with representations of king-sized cola cans. As we hammered into our first number, 'TV Eye', I could see the disgust that Iggy felt at having to perform on what was basically a soft drink commercial billboard. Now, we knew that Pepsi Cola were the sponsors for the two New Zealand festival shows because the Barnestorming tour itinerary had 'Pepsi presents', written all over it and their corporate symbol stamped on the cover. But what we hadn't realised was that we were expected to perform and play our music with those fucking monstrous cans of soda at our shoulders and a stupid, presumptuous advertising slogan for a backdrop. None of that stuff had been present during the soundcheck. It must have been hauled up just before the first band was due to play by the devious cola stage-hands.

Iggy was far from happy. After bringing 'TV Eye' to an end he pointed up at one of the banner cans and screamed into his microphone, "See that? I'd rather drink my own piss than touch that vile shit."

This appealed to the crowd's innate sense of anarchy and they let out a roar of agreement as Iggy bullied and whipped us into a searing extraordinary performance of 'Five Foot One' which jumped and jolted like no version we'd ever delivered before.

After each song of the set, Iggy had a new observation to share with the audience about our sponsors.

"If those fuckers are the voice of a new generation, then I'm glad I'm a fuckin' old fart!"

"Yeah, Iggy, you tell those corporate assholes what's what," the crowd seemed to be baying back in its own wild-assed communal fashion. "We're on your side, Iggy, man... Let 'em have it."

The crowd's approval of Iggy's stance pushed him onto new heights.

"Those evil sons of bitches at fuckin' Pepsi want to rot your guts and brains with their poisonous shit. They want to fill your veins full of their pus, filth and garbage, and turn you into non-thinking bloated fucking consumers. Well, fuck them! Fuck them! Fuck them..." Then he

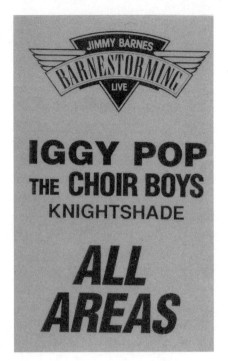

turned to us. "Okay, motherfuckers, give me 'Search and Destroy', and pointing to the Pepsi backdrop, Iggy added, " 'Cos that's what I'm gonna do to the assholes who expect me to sing with that on my stage."

It was classic, old-style Iggy Pop. But the greedy corporate assholes that Iggy had been referring to throughout our set were by now choking on their drinks in the VIP box up in the main stand and had decided they had had enough of his insults. My God. Didn't this Iggy Pop maniac realise he was bad-mouthing a world renowned institution? A multinational, multimillion dollar corporation and a symbol of the free West. This was a power not to be trifled with. The word went out to shut up that ungrateful foul-mouthed fiend.

With a couple of songs to go 'til the end of the set, a middle-aged man dressed in the full corporate regalia of Pepsi logo baseball cap, T-shirt and tracksuit arrived at the side of the stage, notably devoid of the bootlicking smile he had been exhibiting all day. I could see he was shouting something at Henry that our trusty TM didn't appreciate, 'cos Henry shouted right back and started to push the cola rep off the stage. That rep would have been torn to pieces by the crazed audience who were, by that time, acting like a pack of badly treated underfed Rottweilers. But, just before Henry could throw him over the edge, a couple of stage-hands intervened and pulled them apart. They parlayed for some time before our TM finally gave a concessionary nod and the Pepsi prat left our stage of his own volition.

With the penultimate number of our performance finished, Iggy was just about to go into another anti-Pepsi tirade when he spotted Henry waving him across to talk. Henry whispered into Iggy's ear. This turned out to be the equivalent of lighting the fuse wire of a stick of dynamite. Iggy strutted back to centre-stage, pointed directly up at the horrified executives in the stand and shouted at them, "Fuck you, you fuckers! Corporate pieces of shit... Fuck you all."

Paul counted us into 'I Gotta Right', and as the searing waves of sound rolled over the ecstatic crowd, the fuse was done and Iggy exploded. Leaping onto one of the Pepsi banners and hanging on tight with his arms and legs, he began swinging on it to and fro, building up momentum 'til the banner's rope fixings gave way and the whole thing came crashing down with Iggy underneath it onto the stage.

Hell, I thought, what next? I was right – Iggy wasn't through yet. Jumping up from the drum riser onto Andy's pseudo-Marshall stack, he stood there a while with his back to the audience and his arms raised feeling McCoy's sledgehammer guitar on the soles of his feet. Then, with a rebel yell, he swan-dived off the stack onto 'THE VOICE OF A NEW GENERATION' backdrop and clawed onto it, kicking and screaming and willing the whole fucking thing to the ground.

This was Iggy as Jesus, clearing the money lenders out of the temple. Those corporate fools had desecrated his stage with their foul lies and hypocrisy, and now Iggy was determined to make them pay. Iggy's explosion started a chain reaction like rolling thunder across Athletic Park. There were bottles and cans flying in all directions. Threats and counter-threats and the tangible taste of violence in the air. A large number of fist fights suddenly erupted in the audience. The cola-police turned up on stage, en masse, in their distinctive PepsiSwag uniforms, to attempt to prevent more damage to their precious advertising material. They found, instead, that they had to do battle with our rough and ready road crew. Never one to miss out on enhancing a volatile and dramatic moment, Andy kicked over his amplifiers and did his best to lay out one of the invading Pepsi Army with his guitar.

And all the while, Iggy was still desperately swinging on the backdrop, exerting all his power and resources towards its destruction. Finally, Henry decided it was time to retreat while we still had a chance of making it back to the dressing room in one piece. Jos prised Iggy off the backdrop and virtually carried him to safety while Andy, Paul, Seamus and I spotted an escape route past the warring factions and bolted for it. In the sanctuary of our dressing room, we looked at each other and fell into fits of euphoric laughter.

"Let Jimmy Barnes fuckin' follow that!" was Iggy's final comment as we boarded the bus for our ride back to town.

The following evening, after our departure from Wellington for the White Heron Hotel overlooking a scenic stretch of water in Auckland, two lawyers representing the Pepsi Cola Corporation made a visit to Henry's room. First, they registered a complaint in strong terms about Iggy's anti-Pepsi comments and the near-destruction of their advertising hoardings at the Wellington gig. Then, they gave an ultimatum concerning our Mount Smart Stadium show in Auckland the next day. If there was any reoccurrence of the "vile, inflammatory and patently untruthful comments" about their product and

attempted destruction of their property, they would sue Iggy Pop for defamation and criminal damage. To this end, they told Henry that they would be sending a camera crew on behalf of the company to film our show to use as evidence if Iggy ignored their warning and it came to a court case. Henry calmly told them that he would discuss the situation with his employer. He promptly made his way to Iggy and Suchi's room to relay the news and discuss the implications of this development.

I always thought that real rock 'n' roll and big business didn't mix, and here was my proof. Safe, soulless, corporate-approved performers and performances were what they wanted; Iggy wasn't conforming and playing their game. They had reacted in the only way those people know how, and that's to shut the upstarts up with ultimatums, threats and men in grey suits talking legal action.

On the afternoon of the Mount Smart show, as a hired coach wound its way up to the stadium carrying band and crew, Iggy was faced with a stark choice: either to be consistent in his dissent and repeat his already legendary – via the press and public present at the Wellington gig – unfettered anti-Pepsi performance with its legal and professional consequences, or submit to the pressure from the corporate lawyers and lay himself open to the accusation of being a cop-out and a pussy. Tough decision.

As we killed time in the dressing room, drinking coffee and warming up for the show, I could sense that even Iggy, or rather Jim Osterberg, didn't know how Iggy Pop would react once he was in full flight up on the stage. It could go either way. The third number of the set gave us our answer.

'Til that point, Iggy had strutted and shaken and delivered his usual high energy exhibition, minus his observations about our sponsors and their product. Then, half-way through the song 'Weird Sin', he danced his way up to the Pepsi banner at stage right and started to shadow box with his back turned to the crowd. His boxing became faster and wilder; as we moved into the middle section of the song and Andy took his guitar solo, Iggy seemed to be working himself up for some dramatic move. I figured it was just a matter of seconds before he launched himself at the offending banner, dragged it down, stomped on it, and to Hell with the consequences. I was proved wrong.

As his punches got closer and closer to that banner, he suddenly let out a scream that sounded for all the world like that of a wild, caged animal and turned and ran to grab his mike stand in the middle of the stage. Iggy began smashing the stand into the monitors, the amplifiers, and then the drum riser, trying desperately to give release to his obvious frustration. Finally, he flung the mike stand to the floor, just a couple of feet in front of where I was standing. It bounced back up off the stage like a speeding missile, and I ducked just in time to prevent it smashing into my face where it would have caused a serious injury. It was a near miss but I wasn't really angry with Iggy's action. I understood how he felt. Anyway, dodging and weaving around his mike stand antics had been an integral part of the gigs from day one.

For the rest of the show, Iggy became a stern master, berating and goading the band to higher ground. It was an intense affair. When it finally came to an end, Iggy ignored the cries for an encore and we made the walk back to our dressing room to wind down on New Zealand chilled white wine. I guess Iggy's normal operatic devotion to duty did not stretch to a costly court case and a large pay-out to a seemingly paranoid multinational. I didn't blame him for showing restraint. He had already made his point in dramatic fashion at our previous gig. Once again, this exhibited evidence of a wiser, maturing Iggy Pop.

There was one small act of defiance still to come. As Seamus uncorked a second bottle of vino, the Pepsi lackey who Henry had almost chucked off the stage in Wellington came through the dressing room door, re-equipped with his bootlicking tendencies and carrying an armful of cola merchandising: identical Pepsi logo T-shirts, caps and running trousers to the ones he was modelling.

"To show there's no hard feelings, I've brought these over for you all," he said.

No-one uttered a word back. We just stared at him, bringing an unmistakable look of intimidation to his face.

"Yeah... Well... I'll just put them down here, shall I?" He put the advertising material on a chair and then handed what looked like a small box of chocolates to Henry. It wasn't chocolates. "It's a video of your show," he explained. "Looks like we won't be needing it now, so we thought you might want it as a souvenir of your New Zealand visit."

Henry refused to take the gift off him, and told him to put it on top of the pile of Pepsi stuff.

As soon as he left the room, Iggy snarled, "Get that load of shit outta here."

Andy and Paul jumped up, grabbed the bundle and dropped it unceremoniously onto the grass outside. The Pepsi Weasel looked round to see his offerings spread out on the ground with Paul stamping on them and Andy attempting to get his dick out and cover them in piss. I had a better idea. I pulled out my trusty cognac bottle from my gig bag, walked over to the pile and ordered McCoy and Garristo to desist. Then, pouring a small amount of brandy over the clothing, I took a match from Andy, lit it and dropped it onto the cognac-soaked swag. Within seconds, we had a nice little blaze going.

Seamus came out and spotted a perfect opportunity: putting on his best Buster Keaton stone face and a Kiwi accent, he walked over to the outraged Pepsi rep and asked, "You wouldn't go get us some shrimps to put on our barbie, would ya mate?"

BIRTHDAY

At the half-way point of the two week sojourn in Australia during which the final shows of the Instinct world tour would be played out, a dispute had arisen that threatened to sour relations between the band and Iggy and his management.

We had reached Brisbane and were hunkered down at the Hilton hotel. Andy, Paul, Seamus and myself were sitting around McCoy's room trying to come up with a solution to our dilemma after a so-so gig at a sardine-can-solid, hot 'n' nasty club in the suburbs. It was a contractual matter. During the rehearsal stage, pre-tour, we had each received identical tour contracts from Iggy's management people, Collins and Taylor, laying down conditions, specifying weekly pay, p.d.s and length of service required. There was also a clause dealing with downtime.

Downtime is a period of time during the course of a tour when a band or individual artist is not engaged in playing shows, and therefore not actively earning money. In layman's terms, it's a vacation; a break from touring, usually of more than four days duration.

Now, of course, during the Christmas period, there was a two week stretch of non-gigging that lasted from the final British pre-Christmas tour date 'til the first concert in Europe early in the New Year. In the contract, these 14 days constituted downtime and, as such, we would receive only half pay for this period. I remember having thought, on reading this, that it seemed a little mean as by that stage we would have been on the road for some five months solid with still another two months of touring to go. There was no other downtime involved and it would be Christmas. But, hey! I didn't want to blow the gig by making waves and becoming unpopular before I'd even played a single show. So, I said to myself, c'est la vie, and kept schtumm.

Not everyone played it the same way. Seamus had worked in a touring capacity with Iggy previously, and therefore felt more confident about questioning these kinds of contractual details. He got on the phone after clocking this half-pay clause during rehearsals, and claimed that Collins and

Taylor had agreed then to pay the band full wages for the two week holiday. He said that C & T had listened to his arguments and eventually agreed with his conclusions. "Okay," they said. "You gotta point... After all, it's Christmas."

Fine, thought Seamus. Thing was, when we checked our bank accounts for downtime pay, it turned out that only half the amount was dished out, contrary to what had been promised. What's more, Henry had just informed us that the management would be holding back a $1,000 each from our final wage, supposedly to cover any unpaid hotel bills or other expenses that may have accrued over the previous few weeks. I, for one, had paid all my bills as I'd gone along. Coming on top of what we now perceived as a broken verbal contract, this had left us angry and spoiling for a fight.

This was a pity as the Australian tour had got off to a great start. Landing in Melbourne proved a welcome relief after the politics and Pepsi foolishness of our two gig New Zealand stint. Waiting to meet me on our arrival at the airport, was Nick Seymour, my bassist friend from the band Crowded House, who insisted I jump into his cool 60s Falcon American motor for a tour of the city.

After a bit of sightseeing, we drove over to his house in the Bohemian artists and musicians quarter of Melbourne, St Kilda. There, Nick, his brother Mark from the Australian group Hunters and Collectors, along with Mark's girlfriend Libby made me a superb welcoming dinner of shark steaks washed down with surprisingly good Australian wines. Nick's house was fine; a kind of Art Deco pre-war gaff with a studio area to paint and draw. Like Iggy, Nick was a keen painter and was responsible for Crowded House's excellent cover artwork, stage backdrops and props. On his easel sat another design for a future House album, along with individual photos of the band that he would work from to achieve life-like representations in paint of Neil Finn, Paul Hester and himself, the three full-time members of Crowded House.

It was a beautiful evening, balmy but not sticky, and the perfect weather for a bit of clubbing. The bunch of us jumped into Nick's Falcon and after picking up Andy McCoy from the Iggy Pop band's hotel, the Southern Cross, drove on to a series of Melbourne clubs to dance and drink, get loose and flirt with the local goddesses.

I knew Nick would get a buzz out of meeting larger-than-life McCoy, and the two hit it off straight away, Nick being specially impressed when Andy winged a free margarita cocktail deal for our party from a club barman who was promised a free pass to our show for every drink we received. By the end of our stint at that club, McCoy had 25 strangers' names to remember to put down on our guest list for the following day's gig. Strangely enough, it was the only time that Andy didn't forget or deliberately renege on that kind of loose arrangement.

The gigs themselves were cool. That first Melbourne Festival Hall appearance proved a post-Christmas performance high point. Our further concerts in Adelaide, Canberra and Sydney were all sonically deep, with each one possessing its own easy chemistry.

But there, in McCoy's hotel room on that hot Brisbane night in February, Seamus's perceived broken verbal contract and the intended $1,000 withholding had shattered our goodwill and high spirits, and threatened to rain on our final parade. This sore point had been festering for a while so Paul had called a band meeting to find out how we each felt about the situation, and to try to reach an agreement on some kind of unified band stance.

Despite the negative overtones, this, in itself, was a positive development. It showed how close we had become as a band since the 'I-myself-me, self-interest rules' early stage of the Instinct tour. This was Andy, Paul, Seamus and myself working as a team, concerned about fairness for each other, and deciding to fight our corner together despite the damage this could do to our individual working relationships with Iggy. We had finally become comrades.

Seamus was adamant that Collins and Taylor had guaranteed on the phone that full pay would be received over the downtime period.

"Are you sure you didn't misinterpret what they said to you," I asked him.

"No, Alvin," Seamus answered. "I know what they said and that's that."

"Yeah, and anyway, what about this $1,000 shit they're pulling on us?" Paul added. "We've all paid our bills and they know it... Do they think we're fuckin' stoopid or somethin'?"

This was the road's end of a seven month intense tour; I knew at this stage of the game, perceptions could be warped, unimportant matters turned into crises, and raw fatigue and alcohol/chemical abuse could be at the bottom of why we felt so strongly about this matter. Yet, it did seem to me that we had a genuine grievance, and that the only way we were going to do something about it was to take some drastic action. I decided to speak up.

"Okay, I guess we all feel strongly about this so I suggest if we're serious about getting something achieved we do what aggrieved workers have traditionally done when other means have failed."

"What's that?" asked Paul.

"Withdraw our labour," I said.

Shit! There I was in a $400 a night suite at the Brisbane Hilton with a cognac in one hand and a Cuban cigar in the other coming on like some kind of renegade far-left trade unionist. This paradox had not slipped my notice but, after all, I was a member of the Musicians' Union, and had voted all my life (and have continued to vote) for the Labour Party of Great Britain, so why would my environmental circumstances make any difference to my beliefs? Fuck it, I thought, this is a serious issue, a matter of principle.

"Yeah," I reiterated, "withdraw our labour... You know, go on strike."

Andy loved the anarchic sound of that. "Yeah, man. Cool. Let's march over to Henry's room now and tell him to inform those fucking managers that we're leaving in the morning unless we're paid the money we're owed tonight."

"Andy," I said, "this isn't the fucking French Revolution. Even if you do bear more than a passing resemblance to that arch-decapitator of the aristos, Robespierre. No need to march anywhere. Let's coolly sit down and write a fax explaining, in clear terms, our position and the consequences of its rejection."

This met with the approval of Paul and Seamus and so, together, we sat down and composed a fax for dispatch to Collins and Taylor in New York City. In it, we explained that we felt let down by the situation concerning less than full payment for those two holiday weeks and the unnecessary withholding of a large sum to cover non-existent bills. As Andy had astutely pointed out earlier that evening, $1,000 can buy a lot of good shit. We finished this off with a threat to pull out of all remaining shows unless this regrettable situation was rectified forthwith, and with each member

of the band signing his name to this virtual declaration of war. Andy wanted to add a death's head skull motif to the bottom of the page but was overruled on the grounds of poor taste.

Together, we walked down the hotel corridor to Henry's room and gave him our hand-written deposition with a request that he fax it to Iggy's HQ on Broadway immediately. Henry glanced at its contents and, for reasons I still can't fully explain just shrugged, said, "okay," and set about doing what he was instructed without any show of concern. Henry was a pretty switched-on TM with his ear close to the ground, so the only thing I can figure is that he had caught wind of our discontent from the band's comments and conversations that week and had anticipated this extreme manoeuvre.

As we dispersed back to our individual rooms, I felt a kind of sadness that things had come to this. It left a bad taste in my mouth and I hoped that when Iggy heard the details, he wouldn't take this matter personally. As far as I was concerned, this was simply a business issue.

The following day, we drove to Coolangatta, a resort town sitting on the sea edge of Australia's spectacular gold coast.

"Good God," observed our sound engineer, Tim Sunderland. "We've travelled thousands of miles just to end up back in bloody Florida."

And indeed, that's just what Coolangatta looked like. Take away the Aussie accents and we could have been in Fort Lauderdale during spring break, complete with beered-up students and testosterone-fuelled bars advertising wet T-shirt contests.

We were due to play a show that night at a wood and plastic dive of a venue called The Patch, a stone's throw from the beach. The thing was, we still hadn't had a fax back from Collins and Taylor. A band meeting was held on the golden sands of Coolangatta beach with Andy supplying the joints, and each of us bringing in a few cans of Castlemaine ale to keep dehydration at bay. You can't be too careful in that kind of weather. The decision had to be made whether to pull out of the gig that night, thus demonstrating that we meant business or, alternatively, play the show and give the management another day to consider our fax and get back to us. After due consideration, we decided on the latter course of action.

"Yeah, let's do this one for Jim," I agreed. "After all, there's still four shows to go over here and if we stick to our guns on those, they're still in jeopardy of losing a pretty penny in concert fees."

"And also," Seamus wisely added, "they can't pull the old 'you didn't give us enough time to get back to you' routine which would make us look like a bunch of hot-headed prats."

That was true.

That night at The Patch, as our set was coming to an end, we each regretted our decision to play for a very different reason. It was a bitch of a gig. A hellish, 110 degree disaster.

The club's power source wasn't up to the demands of a rock 'n' roll backline and every other song the amplifiers and PA would fall silent, requiring the overworked road-crew to run around, turning everything off to prevent a potentially destructive power surge. When the electricity finally returned, sometimes up to three or four minutes later – a lifetime in front of a packed-in, exuberant crowd – they would have to run around again turning everything back on, with the band having to try to pick up where we had left off.

On top of this, my bass guitar radio pack had filled up with sweat and refused to work, and Iggy's microphone decided it would add to the general chaos by making strange high-pitched noises when it wasn't cutting out. Added to this, the temperature on stage made it difficult to breathe, let alone perform and move around – so we had the classic ingredients for a rock 'n' roll nightmare.

Iggy was beyond crazed. Raving and crying with rage and, at one point, when the treacherous mike started to give out those animal-like squeals yet again, threatening. He bounded up onto the stage-side monitor man's sound desk, swinging his mike stand perilously close to the engineer's cranium, and screamed, "I'll fuckin' kill ya…! Y'hear? I'm gonna fuckin' kill ya!"

The ashen-faced monitor man dropped to the ground and hid underneath the desk until, eventually, Iggy desisted from his all-too-serious threats of grievous bodily harm.

A hateful show.

Afterwards, I figured Iggy's knowledge of our planned rebellion must have added to his anger and loathing. But back at our hotel a few hours later, Henry told me over a beer in the bar, that he didn't intend to tell Jim until he received the return fax from Collins and Taylor.

The following morning, we packed our bags and took an Ansett Airlines flight out of Florida – sorry, I mean Coolangatta. Two hours later, we taxied along the runway to our disembarkation gate in Sydney.

I was having a problem with Ansett's cabin crew, and this particular flight had proved to be no exception. I had bought myself an acoustic guitar and carrying case in a music store in Texas during the second North American tour. Since then, I had managed to carry it aboard plane after plane, airline after airline, around Europe, Japan, etc, as hand luggage, without any hassles. But for some reason, since arriving in Australia and travelling Ansett, my benign guitar had suddenly become an instrument of potential disaster.

On trying to board our AN jet bound for Sydney, I was stopped by an officious flight attendant who, in all seriousness told me he considered my six string acoustic a danger to his passengers. This was not the first time I had heard this particular theory since we had started using this airline.

"You're joking," I said.

"No, sir, I'm being deadly serious," he replied.

"Listen… I've carried this guitar on dozens of aircraft, since October last year, without shedding anyone's blood and without bringing a flight to an unscheduled premature end. We're talking a lot of flying here… In the United States, Europe…"

Before I could finish, he dismissed my arguments with a wave of his hand and a smug look. "I don't care, sir. I'm responsible for the safety of these passengers and crew and I say that you cannot bring that into the cabin." This was a classic example of a jumped-up jobsworth exercising his pathetic droplet of power and thoroughly enjoying it. "I have to take it off you and have it put in the hold," he continued.

"But it will get trashed in there with all the other luggage," I protested. "This is a precision instrument… A delicate and finely tuned tool of my trade."

He was distinctly underwhelmed. "I don't care, sir. I say it goes in the hold, so it goes in the hold."

Cunt.

After taking my seat, guitarless, in the business class section, a perky, smiling stewardess came over to me and asked what band I played for.

"The Bachelors," I snapped back. "You know, three laid back, pipe-smoking, turtle-necked lads from Ireland. We were big in the 60s. Had a hit titled 'Diane'."

"Oh, you were my mother's favourites," she said in all seriousness. "Which one's Declan? My mum used to fancy him."

"The weird-looking geek over there," I said, pointing out Iggy, whose dyed blonde hair was sticking out in all directions north through south, with the result that he looked even more freakish than usual.

"That's Declan...? He's not what I expected."

"I know," I said, "but that's what 20 years of addiction to PCP and rubbing-alcohol can do to a man... Horrific, isn't it?"

The stewardess dropped her smile and suddenly got philosophical. "It's sad. It's really sad what people have to go through in your line of business, isn't it?"

"Amen to that," I said. "Amen to that."

We checked with the desk clerk on our arrival at the Sydney Lebel Town House hotel in the vain hope that a fax would be waiting for us from New York.

"What are they about?" I asked Henry. "Don't they know we're serious about pulling out of the rest of these shows?"

"Look, as soon as I receive a message from the management I'll bring it over," he answered.

"Yeah, well, they'd better have contacted us by tomorrow night or you'll have to cancel your first show," added Paul.

That was tomorrow's problem. That day, we had no show to worry about and 24 hours to entertain ourselves in the beautiful city of Sydney. The Lebel Town House was situated in the King's Cross area of town, a district the equivalent of London's West End or New York's 42nd Street and Broadway: a few restaurants, cinemas and theatres along with a kind of kinky low life vibe.

This was the drug-dealing section of the city, so after having eaten hot 'n' sour soup and beef in oyster sauce at a ramshackle Chinese with Paul, on my return to the hotel, it came as no surprise to find that Andy had been out shopping.

My relationship with Mr McCoy had been a little strained of late. Since that glimpse into the dark side of Andy's character in Japan with the Midnight Emperor incident, I had found it difficult not to be down on him, and had distanced myself from his friendship. I think that he, in turn, felt slighted; he had talked less and less about us working together in another capacity after the Iggy tour was over. Up until Japan, he had been enthusiastic about forming a band with me on our return to LA. By the time we had reached Sydney, he had dropped the idea completely.

On my return to the hotel with Paul, though, there was a message waiting for me at the desk requesting that I stop by Andy's room for a chat and a drink.

"Oh, Alvin, cool. I'm glad you could make it," Andy said on opening his door. "Come on in. I've got a little something for you."

Sitting on his bed was a half-dressed young woman with noticeably long, tanned legs, who turned out to be an old girlfriend of Andy's from his Hanoi Rocks, London days. She was in Australia on a modelling assignment. Sitting on his bedside table, on a small mirror next to a flick-knife (hers), was a good two grams of heroin.

"That was quick," I said. "I've only been out for Chinese food and in that time you've scored a chick and some brown. You know, you really should contact *The Guinness Book of Records.*"

"I don't waste time, man," he laughed. Andy bent down over the mirror and tapped out a line. "For you," he said.

"Andy, you know how I feel about heroin. It's an insidious drug and..."

McCoy interrupted my flow. "Come on, man. Show me we're still friends... Just have a little with me."

There was a subtext to this plea. What Andy was doing was acknowledging our recent difficulties and kind of saying, 'I know you don't fully approve of my ways, but if you do a little of this with me, it'll show that you accept who I am, flaws and all, and the past will be forgotten.'

Something like that, anyway.

Now, I know there will be some of you reading this who will think, 'How pathetic', and perhaps rightly so. But I'd say to you, spend some time in that world of extremes in the perception-warping circumstances of a long global rock 'n' roll tour and then come back and see how much your opinion has altered. It's like looking into a fairground mirror. You know it must be your reflection but, God, how you've changed!

I considered Andy's offer. Despite my distaste for some of McCoy's behaviour, I couldn't help, and still can't help, truly liking the man. He's an original, a unique and all-too-rare splash of vivid colour in an increasingly grey world and anyway... Who was I to moralise, being as big if not a bigger asshole and fuck-up in my own way?

"Okay," I said, "but just a little."

"Sure, sure. I've only knocked you out a small line anyway," he reassured me.

I rolled up an Australian $10 bill, a beautiful note with a painted Aborigine on it, and bent down to do Andy's line. When he turned his back for a second, I blew about three-quarters of the amount off the mirror and snorted up a fraction of what Andy had chopped out for me.

"Cool," Andy said, putting his arms around me. "Now we're friends again."

"Yeah," I agreed, "now we're friends again."

As I walked down the hotel corridor, the sickness came: I had to run at full speed to my room, just making it in time to heave up my partially digested Chinese food into the toilet, thankfully managing not to soil the carpet. Fuck, I thought, when am I going to learn? Fuck, the things I do for friendship.

By soundcheck time the next day, the management fax still had not arrived, and we had informed Henry that there would be no soundcheck and, indeed, no show until an agreement was reached.

"Well, I'm gonna have to tell Jim about this," Henry told us.

"Sure," we said back. "Explain the situation, but please believe that we're not bluffing on this one."

"Okay," he replied, "I believe you."

Just two hours before show-time, the Collins and Taylor fax came through, agreeing to pay us full wages for downtime, and informing Henry that the $1,000 withholding was no longer necessary.

Victory. Our united front had paid off and a very nasty situation had been averted. An extremely relieved TM and band, drove to a suburb of Sydney called Newcastle (Biffa Bacon on Fosters) to play a show that night.

Iggy was travelling separately having done his interview thing at a number of radio stations. The only lingering worry I had was how he had reacted to Henry's report of our rebellion and more importantly, how it would effect Iggy's performance and his interaction with the band. In truth, I was fully prepared for angst, anger and disdain. When Iggy walked into the dressing room, I got my answer.

"How's it goin' fellas ?" he yelled out with a beaming smile. "Let's really fuck these Aussies up tonight with some killer rock 'n' roll."

Well, you figure it out.

Maybe it was grudging respect for our non-compromising stance, or just good politics; but whatever was behind Iggy's unexpected and much-brightened enthusiastic mood, I was glad for it.

That night we blew the roof off that Newcastle venue. We followed it with two equally impressive shows at Sydney's Revesby Roundhouse and Perth's Superdrome.

On 18 February 1989, we took our last flight by Ansett Airlines, by this time renamed Air Nazi by the band and crew, to the location of the Iggy Pop band's final gig of Australia and the Instinct World Tour. Melbourne.

It was my birthday.

After a lazy soundcheck at our St Kilda venue, The Palace, Nick Seymour picked me up in his sturdy Falcon to drive me to the Southern Cross hotel bar where birthday drinks aplenty were bought for me by the rest of the band, Henry and Iggy. This was the first time during the whole tour that I got anywhere near half-drunk before a show. Stoned on McCoy's hash, yes... Half-cut on booze, no. But what the Hell? This was the last show. The final climb and drop of the roller-coaster after a global seven month ride. Backstage at The Palace, the atmosphere brought to mind the last day at school before a long summer holiday. Relief and excitement; but uncertainty about how you were going to fill up all those long empty weeks ahead.

Henry came in to tell us it was show-time for the last time and up on the stage, Paul counted us into 'Instinct', our opening number at the beginning. Now it was our opening number at the end. I wanted it to be a special kind of show but it wasn't. On the scale of one to ten, it was probably a six, but that's how these things go.

A post-show birthday party was thrown for me in the dressing room, complete with a dozen bottles of chilled champagne, hugs and handshakes and a birthday cake with a Gibson Thunderbird bass guitar iced on it, just like the one I had used throughout the tour. We all lined up against the back wall of the dressing room still dripping with sweat and chomping on cake for a final series of band photos taken by Suchi, with my camera.

Iggy draped his arms around my neck and Henry shook up a bottle of Moet et Chandon and sprayed us with it, while Suchi snapped away. I have to confess that not a single photo of that set came out as Suchi had, unfortunately, failed to notice that her delicate thumb was resting on the goddamn camera lens.

Our Melbourne promoter came over to wish me a happy birthday, pushed something into my jacket pocket and winked. I looked down and saw it was a gram bag of cocaine. I didn't want any. I really didn't. At that moment in time, on that first day of my 31st year, I'd had enough. Enough of drugs. Enough of everything. I wanted to go home.

I left the coke for someone else to find.

The next day over breakfast, I said my goodbyes to sound engineer Tim, teks Jos and Mark, lighting man Richard and trusty TM Henry. We all swapped phone numbers and promised ourselves we would get together soon; but I knew it would be a very long time before I next saw any of those faces, and that I would never see some of them again. I surprised myself by getting quite emotional at this thought.

Andy and I ran into Paul and Seamus in the hotel lobby. We joked around, exchanged addresses, hugged and said our goodbyes, before Henry informed us that a cab had arrived to take McCoy and I to the airport.

"Where's Jim and Suchi?" I asked him.

"Don't worry," he said, "they're on the same initial flight as you twos. You'll see 'em at the airport."

Iggy and Suchi were indeed on our flight to Sydney. Thing was, now that the tour was over, they were up front in first class, with Andy and me at the back of the plane in the economy seats.

Management revenge? Perhaps…

On reaching Sydney International Airport, Iggy and Suchi waited for us in the disembarkation area and bought us a farewell foaming, ice-cold cocktail in the airport bar. They were off to Hawaii for an end of tour two week vacation, and would be catching a different flight out, an hour hence. Our United Airlines flight 816, destination Los Angeles, was already being called for boarding over the intercom, and Andy and I gulped down our drinks in preparation to leave.

Iggy suddenly got up, "Listen, fellas, I gotta take a piss so hang around a minute."

"Er… Jim, we have to get to our gate for boarding so don't be long, okay?" I told him.

"Okay," he answered.

Twenty minutes later, Iggy still hadn't turned up, so we had no other option but to sling our acoustic guitars over our shoulders and head off across the airport to board our plane. Andy and I embraced Suchi and gave her a kiss.

"Take care, Suchi and say goodbye to Jim for us," Andy told her, and together we left the bar. We had walked half the distance down a long corridor when, suddenly, a familiar voice boomed out from behind us.

"Safe journey, you rock 'n' roll fuckers!" It was, of course, Iggy.

He was standing at the far end of that corridor waving and smiling and saying goodbye his way. We waved back, then continued our journey through the maze of walkways, escalators and corridors to our departure gate where we boarded our 747 jet and got comfortable for the long flight across the Pacific ocean.

"You know what," I said to Andy as we strapped into our seats. "I think Jim deliberately hung around back there so as not to have to say goodbye to us up close."

"I think you're right," McCoy said. "In fact, I'm sure you're right."

Iggy must have had to say goodbye to hundreds of band members, road crew, managers, business associates and fellow rock 'n' roll travellers over the years, each marking an end and a beginning. As our plane defied gravity with a shrug of its expansive shoulders and climbed for the cool blue sky, I figured I had played my part in that ongoing rock 'n' roll opera. I closed my eyes and fell into a deep, deep sleep.

I woke to hear the captain announce that we would be landing in LAX shortly, followed by a weather report that it was hot and sunny (what a surprise) with an expected temperature of 90 degrees Fahrenheit.

Looking beside me at the vast collection of beer cans, glasses and empty miniature bottles on Andy's flip-down seat table, I rightly guessed that he had not slept at all.

"How long have I been out?" I asked him.

"Oh, hours and hours, man. I kept trying to wake you up to have a drink with me but you just mumbled and went right back to sleep."

"I'm sorry, Andy. I must have been emotionally and physically exhausted. We'll have that drink together later in the week."

I glanced down from my cabin window at the mosaic Spanish-style houses below, with their swimming pools glinting in the afternoon California sun like so many pieces of jade through the smog, and grasped the realisation that I was going home at last.

The taxi from the airport pulled up in front of my West Hollywood apartment. I grabbed my suitcase, paid over the $30 fee, adding another $5 for tip, and walked up the outside stairs to my door. There was a note pinned to it from my wife, welcoming me home and explaining that she had stepped out to get us something for dinner at the supermarket on the corner of 5th and La Brea.

Supermarkets. Apartment. Wife. Buying food for dinner. These were things that had been as distant as dreams for seven months, and they struck me as sounding wonderfully unexciting, mundane and reassuring.

I was finally home. Back in Los Angeles. Back in Kill City, back in my neighbourhood – bandless, musically alone and no longer a threat.

OUTRO

Andy McCoy and I never did get that band together. I visited his Venice Beach apartment a number of times to write songs and make plans, but it quickly became obvious that opiates and serious career moves don't mix. He was back on the brown and it would be a while before he would attempt to tackle that particular problem.

Nevertheless, Andy did eventually put an outfit together, the wonderfully a propos Shooting Gallery. The band included one Paul Garristo on drums. Paul had just finished a tour in Japan, his first since Instinct, with ex-Hanoi Rocks singer turned solo artist Mike Monroe. How the normally astute Paul got talked into joining the madhouse that was Shooting Gallery is still a mystery to me, but join up he did. Together they made one distinctly uninspired and unsuccessful self-titled album for Polygram in 1991, before self-destructing during a North American tour as the opening act for Kiss. If you're wanting to know why, just round up the predictable suspects – drugs, money, women.

Paul Garristo split the band, taking with him bass player Dave Treganna and singer Billy G Bang. Together they became the backing outfit for big-in-Japan guitarist Takashi O'Hashi. This, in turn, led to the formation of a full-time band, the Slum Lords and the release of a record for Toshiba/EMI in 1993, titled *Har-Dee-Har-Har*.

But singer Billy had acquired a nasty little habit from his time with McCoy, and the tensions caused by that malady and the lack of solid success of the Slum Lords project led to Paul Garristo moving on once again. After a brief stay in Japan, he went to Los Angeles, married a Californian girl and joined a Hollywood grunge outfit, Burning Hands.

I ran into Paul while on a reunion tour of North America with the UK Subs in 1997. Having played a show in Richmond, Virginia, we stopped by a central club for a couple of drinks before heading back to our hotel on the outskirts of town. Sitting at the bar sipping a vodka-tonic, was my ex-brother in rhythm. He looked well and was in the process of completing a record with Hands at a Richmond studio. We shared a drink and chatted a while, sharing reminiscences of the Pop tour. Last I heard, he was still playing drums with Burning Hands in the clubs of Kill City. I wish him well.

Meanwhile, Andy McCoy, who had divorced his wife a year or so after Instinct, got remarried. It just so happens that his bride was once the girlfriend of ex-Guns N' Roses guitarist Izzy Stradlin. After falling in love sometime in the summer of 1991, they got hitched in Las Vegas during a break in the recording of the Shooting Gallery album. A new bride, plus the responsibility of having to take custody of his young son Sebastian after the shocking death of his first wife from pneumonia, led to Andy cleaning up his act at a Los Angeles drug rehabilitation clinic in 1992.

A year later he visited me in London. Andy and Angela seemed contented enough and talked of leaving the LA fast lane to set up home in his native Finland. In 1994 he moved to Helsinki and put together Shooting Gallery Mark II with a collection of Finnish musicians which included his original Hanoi Rocks drummer Gyp Casino. Together they toured Scandinavia and made a record for Virgin records in Stockholm. As a testament to his new found sobriety he even played a series of shows for the Rock against Drugs organisation.

This suppression of Andy's true nature could not be sustained indefinitely. Around 1995 I started to hear rumours about his lapse back into the dark stuff. A Finnish friend told me it was common knowledge in Helsinki that both Andy and Angela were dancing the junky two-step again, and getting into debt with all the wrong people. As a result Sebastian had been taken away from them by the social services and put into care.

An ugly development. One which was, unfortunately, confirmed a short time later when Andy phoned me to ask if I'd be interested in joining Shooting Gallery for a tour. At first I put down his slurred speech to the wine he said he was drinking. Suddenly he stopped speaking altogether. I yelled down the phone in an attempt to wake him up. No chance. A classic 'user' nod-out situation.

I placed the receiver on the floor, did some reading for about an hour and a half. When I returned to the phone he was still unconscious on the other end, his laboured breathing quite audible. When finally, he did regain cognisance, I politely declined his offer.

Andy disbanded Shooting Gallery shortly afterwards and recorded a solo record, *Building On Tradition,* for the Scandinavian indie AMT label.

More bad rumours drifted my way. Then, in 1998, I received a call from a Finnish film director who was making a movie about Andy's past and present life. He asked me to meet him at the Groucho Club in Soho. Over lunch he explained Andy had suggested me for an interview for inclusion in the film. I agreed. He said he would arrange for me to fly to Helsinki in a couple of weeks.

The director had some unsavoury information regarding Andy and Angela's personal situation. It seems they had fled from Finland to escape certain parties, leaving a trail of debts and a lot of vexed people behind. They had been living in Bombay for six months, where he had shot a lot of good footage and agreed to rent them a house and pay all their expenses as part of the deal for their full participation in the film. Of course it wasn't long before this expenditure grew in order to support their prodigious narcotic needs, and the poor fool began receiving hourly calls demanding more money or their immediate withdraw from his movie. They had also made enemies of a group of Indian dealers and were worried about reprisals. While Andy was in India, his son Sebastian had been handed over, by Finnish social services, to his British grandparents who had obtained legal guardianship and taken him to the UK. They continue to be responsible for his upbringing and education.

A week later the director called from Finland to tell me Andy and Angela had returned to Helsinki and were about to embark on some more filming before I was due to fly over. He mentioned an idea about a modern day *Romeo and Juliet* scene set in a tower block with Andy on a balcony. I said it sounded interesting, and awaited my air ticket. It never arrived. A few days later I received another call. It seemed the *Romeo* scene had gone badly wrong.

After a fourth floor balcony in a Helsinki tower block had duly been found and Andy positioned in it, an argument broke out with Angela. Andy told her to, "Shut the fuck up!" Angela responded with some choice expletives of her own. Andy climbed onto the outer edge of the balcony and jokingly threatened to jump if she didn't desist. Her harangue continued. Andy slipped and fell to the hard pavement below where he sustained two broken legs. He was lucky he wasn't killed. My trip to Finland was off.

I asked the director to tell Andy I was thinking of him, and if there was anything he wanted or I could assist with, to please call. He said he would pass on my message. He was just off to McCoy's hospital bedside to film him shooting up while still in bondage to leg traction for inclusion in the movie.

I last heard from Andy in mid-1999. One evening I found a message from him on my answering machine. His movie, *The Real McCoy,* had just been released in Scandinavia and he was on his way to a screening at the Berlin Film Festival with the director. He was now out of a wheelchair, his legs on the mend. He left a Helsinki telephone number which he asked me to ring so we could talk in depth on his return from Germany. I tried this number several times to no avail. The final time I got a robotic Finnish voice which I presumed was telling me the number was no longer in service. Pity.

Andy McCoy, as you have no doubt gathered, can be a rake and a rogue and at times, something darker still. But all in all, he has been a generous and true friend to me over the years, and for that I am grateful. What's more, he's a fine guitarist. Please play on Andy, my friend.

After our farewell on that last day in Melbourne, Australia, I fully intended to call Seamus Beaghen, but somehow never got around to it. As I glanced through the British music press, I expected at some point to read about him being involved in some music project or having joined a new band but, surprisingly, there was no information regarding the ex-Iggy Pop band keyboard player and rhythm guitarist.

Then, at my London home some time during 1993, I turned on the TV to watch a new series starring a British comedian named Jack Dee. There on the screen, beneath a hairless head reflecting the studio lights, was Beaghen's unmistakable face. He had copped a weekly gig as Jack Dee's keyboard player, musical director and bandleader. Seamus opened the show with his band and would have a guest spot with such artists as Tom Jones and Elvis Costello.

In 1999, I chatted to him at Iggy's show at the LA2 on London's Charing Cross Road. He looked the same. Shaved head, wrap-around shades, black turtle neck shirt, Doc Martin shoes. He'd given up the Jack Dee gig a couple of years before, and was now playing full time with the critically acclaimed band Death In Vegas.

After the travel and excitement of the Iggy Pop band touring experience, I found it difficult to adapt to day to day life back in Hollywood. Sure, at first it was wonderful not to live out of a suitcase any longer, to have the time to spend with my wife and to follow my own schedule. But inevitably, those post-tour blues set in and I longed for the thrills and spills of the roller-coaster again.

On tour, it's so easy to get used to the rarified air. Your body and mind become geared up for it and when you suddenly have to drop to a lower, slower altitude it becomes hard to breath and function. As a result I became irritable, bored, disagreeable to live with. After a couple of weeks of being unpleasant, I decided extreme measures were called for. I went to the bank, took out a wad of money and flew alone to London. There, I purchased two air tickets as a belated (it was March) extra Christmas present for my father. I took him to see the Pyramids and the enigmatic Sphinx in Cairo and the Valleys of the Kings and Queens in Luxor, Egypt. Those two weeks of Middle Eastern adventure did the trick. They provided the perfect means of decompression. On my return to Los Angeles, I felt relaxed and calm but had reached the conclusion it was time to move on.

I had lived in California for five years and my visits to England with the Instinct tour had only served to remind me of how much I missed London. I'd spoken with Iggy a number of times on the phone regarding a possible gig with him for a Farm Aid appearance and there was some loose talk about his next studio album. But this seemed just talk. There were no hard proposals or definites involved. So when I received a call from the UK from yet another ex-member of Hanoi Rocks, guitarist/singer Nasty Suicide, real name Jan Stenfors, offering me a job in London, I took it.

I exchanged LA for London at the start of 1990. There I set about touring with Mr Suicide's band Cheap and Nasty, with another son of Finland, Timo Caltio, on rhythm guitar and half Native American Indian drummer, Les Riggs. Incidentally, I had already met and got to know quite well both of these musicians from the pool of talent back in Kill City.

After two months of good music press and some happening gigs, we clinched ourselves a deal with China Records. Our first album *Beautiful Disaster* was released in March 1991, followed by more touring in the UK and Scandinavia, via a particularly successful visit to Japan where *Beautiful Disaster* became a top ten record.

During that same year, I got to meet up with a number of my Instinct tour companions. For a Cheap and Nasty Marquee Club appearance in London, I hired the services of drumtek Jos and guitartek Slouch. They were as absurdly funny as ever and it was a joy to work with them again.

Later in the year, I got my manager to acquire me two backstage passes and set off to London's Brixton Academy to see the new Iggy Pop band. They were great. Iggy looked wild and cool in his longer, natural-coloured hair, ripped-up jeans, battle-scarred torso. The band were a collection of young guns from California, friends of Iggy's son Eric, playing a mixture of material from Iggy's then new album *Brick by Brick* and earlier Stooges stuff such as 'No Fun' and 'Raw Power'. In fact, Eric was the first person I ran into backstage. He had replaced Jos as full-time drumtek. After an enthusiastic greeting, he told me his dad knew I was at the gig and wanted me to stop by the dressing room to say hello. So I did.

It was a good reunion. We embraced, talked and drank chilled white wine. He was still with Suchi then, and she looked wonderful in a skin-tight designer dress. I told him how much I liked his new band and he asked me about Cheap and Nasty, and how things were working out for me in

London. Then, Henry McGroggan, still in the trusty TM role, and production manager Mark Edwards walked in and there were more hugs, 'how the devil are you's', and the swapping of recent tour stories.

After an hour or so, it was time to split, and following an exchange of new addresses as both Iggy and I had moved since the Instinct tour, we said our goodbyes again. I headed for home feeling enlivened by Iggy's music and conversation.

Following the termination of the Instinct tour, Iggy got a substantial movie part as Johnny Depp's father in the John Waters movie, *Cry Baby*. He never did take that starring role in the proposed horror flick, *Zombie Cop,* and to my knowledge that movie never got made.

His follow-up album to *Instinct* was the critically acclaimed *Brick By Brick*. Released in 1990, it was Iggy's first piece of product for his new record company Virgin, after a high-profile split from A&M. Produced by Don Was of Was Not Was, *Brick By Brick* utilised a bunch of top session men such as Waddy Wachtel on guitar and Charlie Drayton on bass, as well as star guests such as Slash and Duff McKagan from those Guns N' Roses. Iggy also teamed up with singer Kate Pierson of the B52s for the hit single from the album, 'Candy'.

This was followed by the inevitable promotional tour which more or less took Iggy up to 1992. Writing songs with his new touring guitarist Eric Schermerhorn, Iggy checked back into the studio to lay down tracks using the backing band I'd seen at the Brixton Academy. Iggy and his young band, along with notable guests Henry Rollins and Lisa Germano, produced from these sessions the killer album *American Caesar.*

Following its release in '93, Iggy once again took to the road – his true home – in support of the record. During that international tour, he played London a couple of times and made a headline appearance in Stratford-on-Avon at the summer 1994 Phoenix Festival. Each time, I was either out of the country or unable to make the shows due to some prior professional engagement.

Cheap and Nasty released a second album, *Cool Talk Injection,* for the Japanese domestic record label Pony Canyon in early 1994. I ended up spending a lot of time visiting and playing shows in the country of my childhood fascination, Japan. But, as so often happens when a situation seems stable and viable, things changed.

During the fall of '94, despite a third album in the pipeline, Nasty Suicide decided to split from the band that carried half his name, to pursue a love interest in Tokyo. He became a sidekick for his old Hanoi Rocks singer and fully paid-up member of the Iggy Pop rip-off club, Mike Monroe.

Oh well, what the fuck did I expect from someone with a name like Nasty Suicide anyway… Loyalty?

It all turned out for the best: having no music biz interests to take care of, I suddenly had the time and inclination to sit, think and write about those remarkable seven months as a member of the Iggy Pop band. The end result was this book, first published by the now defunct Britannia Press in 1995. My second book, *Destroy* – a personal history of punk rock – was published by the same company the following year.

During the period between the two books, I separated from my wife. I guess the emotional strains that result from being constantly away from a partner finally served to destroy our marriage. We divorced in 1997.

In late 1996, I flew to San Francisco to reunite with the UK Subs. Over a four week period we wrote and recorded in a Haight Ashbury studio. The creative consequence was two albums: *Quintessentials,* for the New Red Archives label, and *Riot,* for Cleopatra Records.

In 1997, to promote the simultaneously released records, we embarked on a six week tour of America. It was good to be on the road again.

I wasn't the only one going through the solemn experience of divorce. During the mid '90s, Iggy became estranged from Suchi, and their marriage became permanently dissolved. I don't know the details; I only know that it's hard to imagine Jim and Suchi as two separate entities after the closeness they demonstrated during my time with them.

The disappointment of Iggy's next studio album, *Naughty Little Doggy,* in 1996, was negated by the huge boost his career received by the prominent inclusion of 'Lust for Life' in the hit movie, *Trainspotting.* As a result, Iggy was super-hip again and his music seemed to grace just about every other advert on the small screen: Nike sports, 'Search and Destroy'; Nissan cars, 'Passenger' and Grolsch beer, 'I'm Bored'.

On the acting front, Iggy has starred on the big screen in *The Crow II,* and appeared in an episode of TV's *Deep Space Nine.*

Iggy's latest record, the excellent *Avenue B.,* was released in 1999. It was at his gig in London on the tour to promote this album, that I caught his performance at the LA2. That gig convinced me that Iggy is getting better with age, tearing up the stage as never before with a new degree of self-confidence and self-possession.

I still believe Iggy Pop to be the finest performer in rock 'n' roll. Forget those moneyed, slack-assed Rolling Stones. Forget the new pack of Iggy imitators who have mastered the behaviour and poses but are utterly devoid of the fearless heart and attitude. There are only two Iggy Pops and one of them is James Newell Osterberg Jr.

Long may they both reign.

SELECTED DISCOGRAPHY

SINGLES

The Iguanas • 1965
Mona / I Don't Know Why

The Stooges • 1969
I Wanna Be Your Dog / 1969

The Stooges • 1970
Down on the Street /
I Feel Alright

Iggy & the Stooges • 1973
Search and Destroy /
Shake Appeal

Iggy Pop • 1977
China Girl / Baby

Iggy Pop • 1977
Sister Midnight / Baby

Iggy Pop • 1977
Success / The Passenger

**Iggy Pop & James
Williamson** • 1978
Kill City / I Got Nothin'

Iggy Pop • 1978
I Got a Right / Sixteen

Iggy Pop • 1979
I'm Bored / Africa Man

Iggy Pop • 1979
Five Foot One / Pretty Flamingo

Iggy Pop • 1980
Loco Mosquito / Take Care of Me

Iggy Pop • 1981
Bang Bang / Sea of Love

Iggy Pop • 1982
The Passenger / Nightclubbing

Iggy Pop • 1982
Run Like a Villain / Platonic

Iggy Pop • 1986
Cry for Love / Winners
and Losers

Iggy Pop • 1986
Real Wild Child / Fire Girl

Iggy Pop • 1987
Shades / Baby It Can't Fall

Iggy Pop • 1988
Cold Metal / Instinct

Iggy Pop • 1988
High on You / Squarehead

Iggy Pop • 1989
Living on the Edge of the Night /
The Passenger

Iggy Pop • 1990
Home / Lust for Life

Iggy Pop • 1991
Candy / Pussy Power

Iggy Pop • 1993
Wild America / Credit Card

Iggy Pop • 1994
Beside You / Louie Louie

Iggy Pop • 1994
Louie Louie / Hate

Iggy Pop • 1996
Lust for Life / Sex Machine /
Lust for Life (live) / I Wanna Be
Your Dog (live)

Iggy Pop • 1997
Monster Men / Gorgeous / Etno /
Candy / Bad Luck Blues /
Space Goofs

Iggy Pop • 1999
Corruption / Avenue B

ALBUMS

The Stooges
The Stooges • 1969
1969; I Wanna Be Your Dog;
We Will Fall; No Fun; Real Cool
Time; Not Right; Little Doll

The Stooges
Fun House • 1970
Down on the Street; Loose;
TV Eye; Dirt; 1970; Fun House;
LA Blues

Iggy and the Stooges
Raw Power • 1973
Search and Destroy; Gimme
Danger; Your Pretty Face Is
Going to Hell; Penetration;
Raw Power; I Need Somebody;
Shake Appeal; Death Trip

Iggy and the Stooges
Metallic K.O. • 1974
Raw Power; Head On;
Gimme Danger; Rich Bitch;
Cock in my Pocket; Louie Louie
(Recorded live, USA, 1974)

Iggy Pop
The Idiot • 1977
Sister Midnight; Nightclubbing;
Funtime; Baby; China Girl;
Dum Dum Boys; Tiny Girls;
Mass Production

Iggy Pop
Lust for Life • 1977
Lust for Life; Sixteen;
Some Weird Sin; The Passenger;
Tonight; Success; Turn Blue;
Neighborhood Threat;
Fall in Love With Me

**Iggy Pop
& James Williamson**
Kill City • 1977
Kill City; Sell Your Love;
Beyond the Law; I Got Nothin';
Johanna; Night Theme,
Consolation Prizes; No Sense of
Crime; Lucky Monkeys;
Master Charge